In a world filled with social med
the Christ-centered entrepreneur to struggle in business,
authentic storytelling by the featured authors in *The Joy-Full Entrepreneur: Combatting Business Myths, Armoring Up in Truth* offer hope and ignite active faith for the reader's journey!

Shae Bynes, author of *Grace Over Grind*,
founder of Kingdom Driven Entrepreneur

Why is it that the vast majority of the world's one-percenters are unbelievers? That's upside down! Followers of Jesus are the ones representing the King of all resources, the Lord of all commerce, and the inventor of enterprise. We should be LEADING the world of business, not shying away from it. *The Joy-full Entrepreneur* is speaking powerfully to that truth. Read it and be transformed.

Sarah J. Thiessen, LMFT, LPC,
founder of the Splankna Training Institute

This book is so far beyond just a strategy for being successful. The book felt like I was reading a devotional mixed with attending a therapy session! It's so true that skill is not all that's needed to thrive in life. Often, it is doing the DEEP work of finding our identity in the Lord, learning to believe who He says we are instead of who we think we are, and truly trusting Him that makes thriving possible. The enemy of our souls has so many lies that we've believed about money, ourselves, and this world we live in. I implore you to read this book and let your Creator blow those lies out of the water. Success, joy, and identity are all inside jobs, and those attributes make a solid entrepreneur. Enjoy the wisdom from these authors, knowing they are sharing with you the creme de la creme of the hard-earned knowledge they have acquired in the trials of life.

What took them decades to learn is being shared with us in one succinct manual; what a gift!

Laura Milliken, Healthy Relationship Tik-Tok Influencer, Podcast Host, Master Splankna Practitioner

This book is a moving and descriptive body of writing that centers on overcoming self-doubt. The authors lead the reader on a powerful exploration of seeing every situation in life as divine orchestration that can illuminate a path of self-discovery and victory. Expect this book to cause you to reflect, explore your life story, and encourage you to move forward despite doubts or fears.I am truly inspired by what I read and will continue to use it to reflect on my own life.

Dr. Charryse Johnson, LCMHC, NCC, founder of Jade Integrative Counseling and Wellness and author of *Expired Mindsets*

In a world overflowing with misconceptions about success and faith, *The Joy-Full Entrepreneur* boldly dismantles these myths with scriptural truth and powerful testimonies. This book is an essential resource for entrepreneurs seeking to align their business practices with Kingdom principles, empowering them to break free from limiting beliefs and embrace a joyful, purpose-driven life. Dive in and discover how to arm yourself with the truth and transform your entrepreneurial journey!

Kyle Draper, best-selling author of *Rethink Everything:You "Know"About Social Media and Rethink Everything You Know About Being A "Next Gen" Loan Officer,* video marketing therapist, founder of Content Compounding

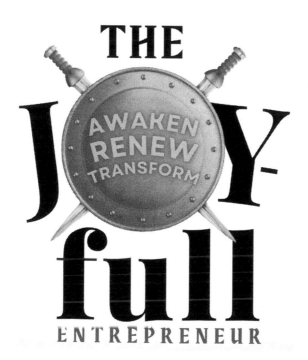

THE J**O**Y-full

AWAKEN RENEW TRANSFORM

ENTREPRENEUR

THE JOY-full

AWAKEN
RENEW
TRANSFORM

ENTREPRENEUR

TAMRA ANDRESS

FOREWORD BY DAYNE KAMELA

F.I.T. in Faith LLC
Virginia Beach, Virginia
Fitinfaithpress.com
Editing: Sharon Miles Frese

ISBN: 978-1-7379022-4-9

Published by F.I.T. in Faith Press
www.fitinfaithpress.com

THIS BOOK IS DEDICATED TO...

all the builders, the apostles, the trailblazers, the founders, and the next generation of leaders...the ones who have a vision to expand the Kingdom of Heaven here on earth. As those who have gone ahead... we refuse to let those behind us falter into the fallacy of the enemy's tactics to steal, kill, and destroy through deception. After all, he is the Father of Lies, so we must be prepared for his schemes. And remember, we are in a fight (not against flesh and blood). And you are a warrior! We pray this book gets you armored up as a front lineman in the marketplace.

Building kingdom business is counter-cultural in every way. Keep your eyes fixed on Jesus, and the Truth will set you free to flourish as a Joyfull-Entrepreneur.

Table of Contents

Foreword: By Dayne Kamela.. xiii

Introduction: By Tamra Andress.. I

1 Remove the Negative Labels Holding You Back *by Bee Andreen* ...9
"You're Not Cut out for Entrepreneurship"

2 Use What You Got *by Tamra Andress*..23
"Money Is Evil"

3 Need for Control *by Christina Blincoe*...39
"You Are in Control of Your Life"

4 Faith-Filled Foundation *by Victoria Ciresi*..53
"If You Build It, They Will Come"

5 The Power of the Wills *by April Foster*...65
"Willpower Equals Success"

6 Made for This *by Elisah McGee* 79
"You Must Be an Expert"

7 Business Is War *by Chris Rickstrew*..91
"You're an Entrepreneur"

8 The Fruitful Life Equals True Success *by Tierney Shirrell*....................105
"The Be-Do-Have Model for Life Success"

9 The Power of the "And": You Are as Multidimensional as
Your Creator *by Brittany Stinson*...115
"You Must Choose One"

10 Deadly Perseverance *by Brittney Tollinchi*..129
"Quitting Is Failure"

11 Follow Jesus and Walk on Water by Ashley Weston 143
"Go with Your Gut"

12 The Power of Authenticity by Dr. Chelsea D. Washington 155
"You Have to Be Someone Other Than Yourself to Succeed"

What Now? 169
Acknowledgments 177
Supporting Resources 178
About the Lead Author 187

Table of Contents (Part 2)

THE BELT OF TRUTH

Victoria Ciresi 53

Brittany Stinson 115

Chelsea Washington 155

THE BREASTPLATE OF RIGHTEOUSNESS

April Foster 65

THE SHOES OF PEACE

Tamra Andress 23

THE SHIELD OF FAITH

Bee Andreen 9

Brittney Tollinchi 129

THE HELMET OF SALVATION

Elisah McGee 79

Chris Rickstrew 91

THE SWORD OF THE SPIRIT: WORD OF GOD

Christina Blincoe 39

Tierney Shirrell 105

Ashley Weston 143

Foreword

"You don't know what you don't know," and that can be the scariest or most dangerous place to be when a full-on attack from the enemy hits you between the eyes.

Growing up, I was a disinterested Christian, attending church since childhood but never truly seeking God through His Word. I prayed and had faith for good outcomes. I had a praying mom and a grandmother who was also a prayer warrior. Yet I was just like my nonchurch friends, involved in parties and drinking. I was an average student, played on the varsity football team, and was passionate about health and fitness, coaching young athletes to improve their strength, agility, and endurance.

Reading books, especially the Bible, never interested me until one Sunday morning when I attended a new church with my family. The pastor's message on biblical success principles piqued my interest and helped me begin my journey of faith. I bought the pastor's book and read it, excited to learn that God had a great plan for my life (Jeremiah 29:11). I started reading more books—mostly secular ones—on success, motivation, and personal growth, discovering a new world none of my friends were interested in. My dad had always encouraged me to read from his library of similar books, but I never took his advice until then.

I became a new person who loved learning, reading, and hearing faith messages. My knowledge of personal growth expanded quickly, and I was excited about this new world. I read the Bible, asked my mom questions, and shared new insights from personal growth literature. I listened to podcasts and motivational speakers and attended workshops and events. For someone who had never picked up a book (other than a school textbook), I was now reading several books a month and sharing what I learned with family and friends.

Then a strange thing happened. My behavior changed in ways my mother noticed but couldn't understand. I was speaking more rapidly and becoming hyper. Long story short, I had a major mental health breakdown and was hospitalized and diagnosed with bipolar disorder I. Although I had never used recreational drugs, the hospital administered strong medications to stabilize me.

Today, I believe I was under a demonic attack, and I was not clothed in the full armor of God. In my pursuit to increase my knowledge and experience in personal development, I had unknowingly opened the door to unseen forces that came against me. Not understanding my authority as a believer or how to stand firm against the devil's strategies, a spirit of fear gripped me. I retreated from God with no power to fight the enemy.

In my own strength, I couldn't fight. My mind was in shambles, and I thought I had lost every bit of my intelligence. The information I had learned so diligently from studying, reading, and listening was gone. Upon leaving the hospital, my doctor said I would need medication for the rest of my life and confirmed that my brain and level of intelligence had suffered greatly. He gave me no hope that my cognitive abilities and intellect would bounce back and warned me that another episode would damage them further.

> **"In my pursuit to increase my knowledge and experience in personal development, I had unknowingly opened the door to unseen forces that came against me."**

Despite the unfortunate news, my mom consistently reassured me that this was not a permanent condition and that healing was possible. She reminded God of His promises in His Word (Isaiah 43:26) and, in her unwavering faith, encouraged me to believe for my total recovery and not allow the experience to define the rest of my life. I began to speak

God's Word and healing over my life, believing that healing was possible for me. My identity, which the enemy had targeted, was rooted in Christ, and I began to fight the good fight of faith and clothe myself daily with the full armor of God.

Through God's grace, His promises in the Word, and the prayers of strong Christians and family who were equipped and armed to stand by me (Ephesians 6:11–18), I was supernaturally healed during a church service just weeks after my diagnosis. God healed me completely and transformed my life. What I thought I had lost intellectually came back, and my capacity to learn quickly and retain knowledge actually improved. It has been over ten years now, and since my healing, I have not needed any medication. I finished my college education and graduated. What the enemy meant for evil, the Lord God Almighty turned around for good (Genesis 50:20).

This healing experience transformed my relationship with God and deepened my confidence in what Jesus can do for those who trust in Him. Six years after my healing, God called me to share my faith on social media. In just four short years, Litwithprayer has reached tens of millions of people around the world with the Good News.

My prayer for you is that this book will help you uncover the lies the enemy has led you to believe and empower you to put on the full armor of God. May it enable you to break free from bondage and step into the fullness of what God has called you to do with your life. God's Word is alive and active, and as you apply it, you will experience greater freedom in your life. "And ye shall know the truth, and the truth shall make you free" (John 8:32, KJV).

God is so gracious, and He has brought many strong Christians into my life, like Tamra Andress, who encouraged me on my journey to reach millions of people around the world through the powerful act of prayer on social media. I am honored to write this foreword to encourage you to know your enemy, whose mission is to steal, kill, and destroy your life and your influence on others. Put on the whole armor of God because, like me, when you are a wounded warrior, you may be called not only to fight but also to help those who need your prayers and your faith in times of spiritual warfare.

"PUT ON THE WHOLE ARMOR OF GOD BECAUSE, LIKE ME, WHEN YOU ARE A WOUNDED WARRIOR, YOU MAY BE CALLED NOT ONLY TO FIGHT BUT ALSO TO HELP THOSE WHO NEED YOUR PRAYERS AND YOUR FAITH IN TIMES OF SPIRITUAL WARFARE."

—Dayne Kamela[1]

---

1 Dayne Kamela is a social media content creator who shares inspiring daily messages around prayer, hope, and encouragement. He is the founder of Litwithprayer, an organization with a mission to help people develop a strong relationship with God through education and tools so they can discover and fulfill their God-given potential.

Introduction by Tamra Andress

A false reality has been created around entrepreneurship. The highlight reels are a figment of our imagination, and social metrics have never been so disproportionate to the legitimacy of a business entity. Systems, structures, and quick-win support courses are being sold by fixed funnels that aren't even rooted in historical data. Technology is moving so fast that any guru proclaiming the next trend or algorithm has fast fame or growth and considers it a fundamental practice, even though it's outdated. Ingrained in our psyche, the commonplace mantras of our youth keep us circling old stories and practices that "must be true" because *x*, *y*, and *z* are still true. Campaigns of a "woke" society have tainted our lens on work ethic, success, ministry, money, sales, marketing, identity, and even the character of Christ. Social isolation has tarnished true mastermind experiences, limited movements, and created loneliness, disillusionment, and depression. The normalized life of "busy" has become our trap—a facade of contentment and peaceful living. The suppression tactics used to "chill" or "have fun" have broken our body's integral structure, thus inhibiting sleep, healthy adrenaline, dopamine levels, emotional and mental stability, intimacy, and relationships. The masks we wear are now so commonplace that litter boxes are in schools, and people are walking around unaware of their genetic makeup. The loudest, richest, most famous, or most followed voices of our time are missing the true *one thing* (Jesus). And some are even using God's name to target Christian audiences to get their next share.

We are being scammed.

It's time we open our eyes. Discernment is a gift from the Holy Spirit. But our world is so loud and "connected" that we have become disconnected from His voice, His Word, and His will.

In fact, we have laid down our armor, and with that, we have laid down our will to fight. We are made to be the strongest fighters. The mightiest warriors. The frontline men. The ones standing on the ramparts, sounding the alarms for others. And yet, we are weary, distracted, and restless—praying for Jesus to come back when He's actually created us for "such a time as this," to build the safe havens, the communal living spaces, the ministries, the businesses, and the solutions that will ethically serve and share and multiply. We are the messengers meant to share the greatest news with all nations to the ends of the earth. To support the least of these instead of marginalizing them. To evoke hope and be light in this dimming place that we call home (for now). Yes, we are but sojourners, as Peter proclaims. But that does not give us the right to sleep our way through or keep ourselves comfortable. The calling everyone is talking about and looking for is a command. And comfort zones are complacent zones that keep you from living up to your fullest potential as a son or daughter of the King.

"Wake up!" I say to His church. "Wake up! And Armor up!"

As followers of Jesus, our role in speaking Truth, walking in love, and making disciples of all nations must include the deep-seated reality of the gospel when it comes to building. The chanting of "kingdom entrepreneurship" or "faith-driven business" or "God is my CEO" doesn't exclude you from the trials and tribulations. It doesn't mean everything miraculously appears at your fingertips each morning. It doesn't mean that floodgates open and clients are jumping to be served by you the moment you open your doors.

> "The calling everyone is talking about and looking for is a command."

Just like Noah, given the vision and word from God, you, too, start with a clean slate, a plot of "land" (even if that now means digital space), and you get to work. And each day you show up to a messy construction site with an often cloudy blueprint that only gets revealed along the way, naysayers who can't comprehend what in the world you are doing, and heated moments that will challenge your gall. This would be the perfect place for a "But God" insert. . . . However, I think it's more appropriate (with our cultural climate, the context of this book, and what's at stake) that I tell it like it is: the "But Satan" situations that will most likely transpire as the precursor to a move of God will be what destroys the vision, weakens the contractor, and causes leaders, teams, warriors, and even ministers to throw in the towel.

The Father of Lies has masked us—at times literally but most often figuratively.

"HE WAS A MURDERER FROM THE BEGINNING, NOT HOLDING TO THE TRUTH, FOR THERE IS NO TRUTH IN HIM. WHEN HE LIES, HE SPEAKS HIS NATIVE LANGUAGE, FOR HE IS A LIAR AND THE FATHER OF LIES"

(John 8:44)

Let me clarify so that you aren't immediately shutting down the shop and running back to your quiet life of mediocrity or even misconstruing the aforementioned references as a bleak lens to pursuing your God-given purpose, dream, desire, vision, or whatever you want to call it. We do serve a mighty God. One who can and will do exceedingly and abundantly above all that we ask, think, or imagine according to the power that works in us (Ephesians 3:20–21). The Holy Spirit is our helper, and we have many advantages over any and every ploy of the enemy. So let me breathe hope on the same page so as not to give Satan an ounce of glory.

God may give you a pristine, clear blueprint from start to finish. I hope He does, and I'm certain that in your actions, He will co-labor with you to create clarity on where to go and what to do next. But God is not a crystal ball carrier; that's for the psychics and mediums we're instructed to avoid. So why do you keep asking for clarity?

You may also have a quick rise into business "success" (whatever that definition is to you but, of course, through the lens of the Lord). But faulty foundations and lack of structure will not support the longevity of what God wants to do fully unless you build effectively, partnering with other contractors who can carry the load with you. This is the Body of Christ. I've only ever known one one-man show that worked, and even He was a triune guy.

Things will 100 percent miraculously show up to resource, surprise, and delight you along the way. But, remember, it's your faith in action, your "stepping out of the boat" with eyes fixed on Jesus, that will keep you safe, not the "resource" itself.

Remember, stay strong and courageous because you may also have to trust devoutly for decades until the rain fully comes. And even then, you may lose friends, family, and everything you once knew to enter into the next plan and season God had prepared for you before you were born (Psalm 139:13). Insert the rainbow because we serve a sovereign God, and His promises are still true today.

The truth is building anything that will last and leave a legacy while transforming hearts takes a lot of hard work. They say it takes "blood, sweat, and tears," and I can attest to all three (honestly, often daily) in varied seasons of construction and development through nearly two decades of entrepreneurship and tens of thousands of lives touched through many business endeavors. Ultimately, our dreams should become our labors of love. While His yolk is easy and His burden is light—and it's always "grace over grind" as my spunky sister Shae Bynes reminds us in her book—it's clearly stated: "Unless the Lord builds the house, the builders will labor in vain" (Psalm 127:1).

So, to understand how to combat enemy tactics that are sent to destroy the good thing that has been seeded inside of you to grow and build, you must establish the truth that even partnering with a wonderful, anything-is-possible, perfect God will most certainly still require surrender, sacrifice, obedience, and diligence. This is because God is more concerned about shaping you than building something that breaks you. The gifts you receive amid your construction, crafting, and abiding are the beautiful fruits of self-control, patience, and, surely, added measures of wisdom. But He gives these *not* to build you up for yourself but to build you up for Himself, which allows you to bless others and bring them into Him.

But I see you. Yes, you. . . . You're reading this, like, "Ya, ya, I know." You're one of the secret-closet Bible scholars, one of the prayer warriors who practices the Sabbath and fasts regularly. You've gotten clarity from Christ, and you know it isn't easy out there in the heat of the day, day after day, but you show up with joy and peace and faith that is larger than a mustard seed. Ya,

> "...God is more concerned about shaping you than building something that breaks you."

you likely already classify yourself as a *joy-full entrepreneur* too, don't you? You don't even need to go to one of those conferences to get motivated again. You wake up on fire for the mission of Christ. Well, good! You are in the right place too.

So whether you are fearlessly fighting or freely flying, both require combat. Both require the armor of God. Both require (as my strong friend Amberly Lago shares so eloquently) grit, pace, and perseverance.

As you delve into the stories shared in this anthology, this compilation of revelations about God's Truth, you will arm yourself with deeper wisdom and powerful weapons. Imagine as you meet with each warrior that you're stepping onto their personal battlefield, the very place God has asked them to conquer and build. Their testimonies may resonate with you, or they might seem far off from any attack you've witnessed thus far, but stand guard, soldier. This is a time to equip yourself and recognize that the armor being passed to you may not be the right fit for your specific battle. But the honor isn't in the armor you wear, it's in the will to fight and the knowledge that will cement as wisdom when you try it on for size and recognize the unique stature you've been gifted—

the setup of a lifetime that is occurring as God anoints the one being sent: you. Moreover, you may meet a fellow warrior along the way who needs that exact tactic, that new wisdom, that specific weapon for their warfare, and your due diligence in this read will be a critical key for them later.

Ultimately, you may not be throwing stones like David. You may not be building a boat like Noah or a temple like Solomon. But we are all fighting a spiritual battle, not against nonbelievers or team members or family or clients—but against the enemy.

"FOR WE DO NOT WRESTLE AGAINST FLESH AND BLOOD, BUT AGAINST THE RULERS, AGAINST THE AUTHORITIES, AGAINST THE COSMIC POWERS OVER THIS PRESENT DARKNESS, AGAINST THE SPIRITUAL FORCES OF EVIL IN THE HEAVENLY PLACES."

(Ephesians 6:12, ESV)

In each section of this book, you will read the battle plans and weapons used by other warriors. And at the end, you will "get dressed" in the Ephesians 6 armor of God and construct your own battle plan, moving forward to combat the myths and claim the Truth.

 The Belt of Truth

 The Breastplate of Righteousness

 The Shoes of Peace

 The Shield of Faith

The Helmet of Salvation

 The Sword of the Spirit: Word of God

As a kingdom builder, pioneer, leader, and soldier for Christ, consider this your clarion call. No more hiding in the shadows. No more trying to build alone. An army of one doesn't define an army at all.

Together, let's continue to confront the lies being broadcasted daily. We are the mighty messengers of Truth. And this book will help you create a battle plan to stand up once and for all against the tactics of the enemy that goad you to quit or stay quiet—both of which are detrimental to God's blueprint for you and His ultimate battle plan. We fight not to win but as proclaimed victors because He has already won. Now He's co-laboring with us for His bride, a.k.a. His church, a.k.a. His people! March on *Joy-full Entrepreneur*.

"FINALLY, BE STRONG IN THE LORD AND IN THE STRENGTH OF HIS MIGHT. PUT ON THE WHOLE ARMOR OF GOD, THAT YOU MAY BE ABLE TO STAND AGAINST THE SCHEMES OF THE DEVIL"

(Ephesians 6:10–11, ESV).

1

Remove the Negative Labels Holding You Back

By Bee Andreen

The Lie
"You're Not Cut out for Entrepreneurship"

Howdy! I'm Bee, your integrative business coach and personal cheerleader. I specialize in helping highly sensitive entrepreneurs build confidence and resilience in business. If you've ever been teased about your tenderhearted traits, then you're in the right place. Highly sensitive people possess God-given strengths that are often overlooked and undervalued during their formative years. Your godly sensitivities and personality traits are likely what drew you to entrepreneurship, but it's crucial to distinguish these from ungodly emotional blocks as you step into your endeavor. For example, someone with keen attention to detail may feel easily overwhelmed and desperate to control everything because they recognize nuances others don't. This illustrates both a godly sensitivity and a related emotional block.

You may be tempted to disguise or suppress your sensitivities in the business world, unsure of how these traits might impact your success and earning potential. This is a sign that emotional blocks may be limiting you from functioning in your full, godly identity.

Before I share my story, I want to congratulate you on your yes! Embracing an entrepreneurial calling can feel exciting and intense. On one hand, you have a strong sense of God-given direction as you recognize your spiritual gifts. On the other hand, stepping out in faith with your time, money, and effort can feel far outside your comfort zone, even if you are certain of who He's asking you to become. Fear not; success and, more importantly, sustenance are built on courage, which is really just a willingness to continue saying yes to Him.

As you're stepping through this exciting process, you'll need this simple prayer for overwhelming days: "Father God, pause and stretch my time." This prayer was given to me in the early stages of my business journey and has encouraged me through what I call the "nope, not today" days. These are the moments when you would rather stay in bed, with the covers pulled over your head, hiding from His requests, when unappealing steps are required. It's critical to have a routine and a simple prayer like this one as you build your new venture, especially while also maintaining your current responsibilities.

Buttoned-up but Misaligned: Years of Experience with Zero Self-Worth

Sometimes, I laugh audibly when I think about God's wonderful and, at times, frustrating sense of humor. They say hindsight is twenty-twenty (whoever "they" are), referring to the clarity gained after stepping through unplanned challenges. Growing an impactful godly business is no different. Believe it or not, I started my first business equipped with seventeen years of business experience and still felt completely lost, plagued by the same question many new entrepreneurs have: "Where do I begin?"

I had invested seventeen years building my career within the walls of my family's oilfield service and supply business. During that season, I was fortunate to gain valuable insight into managing a product- and service-based business, but I had a blind spot. I had never started a business from scratch and, quite frankly, didn't have any desire to.

However, God had other plans for me. He knew my self-worth was entangled in the assumptions I frequently encountered during my early twenties that left me feeling offended. The phrase "must be nice to have Daddy's money" was a judgment that struck me with shame. Yes, people actually said this to my face and even whispered it to others behind my back. This judgment led me to suppress my capabilities, talents, and ambition to avoid threatening those who believed I had some sort of unfair advantage or head start. It also caused me to assume that no matter how hard I worked, I would never be seen or respected in the business world as a woman. Ironically, it was my mother who profoundly influenced my early wisdom concerning business ventures and money management.

> "I had never started a business from scratch and, quite frankly, didn't have any desire to."

In addition to my "Where do I begin?" problem and the misconceptions about my self-worth, I also faced another hurdle. I was a divorced, thirty-year-old, self-supporting, single mother of two small children, attempting to recover from extensive abuse that, at the time, just felt like rejection. I tried desperately to tuck in my "not enough" tag so nobody would recognize how badly I was suffering, but at that time, my identity was defined almost entirely by my struggle.

Though I was equipped with a multifaceted business background, I didn't believe in myself or my capabilities because I was routinely discounted and negatively labeled by the person who once promised to love and protect me.

Dressed for Success: A Shield of Faith and a Rhinestone Microphone

Hopefully, I've adequately described the woman I was before God gave me a new name, a new wardrobe (wearing only His labels), and a new purpose. I had never aspired to hold a professional title or be a savvy businesswoman or successful entrepreneur. When I was little, all I wanted to be was a devoted wife and bread-baking mother, the kind that sews, cooks, crafts, teaches, and plays. Yet, there I was . . . fumbling my way through roles I didn't want, in a life that didn't go as planned. I want to point out, however, that my story isn't uncommon. You can count on Him to bring you to and through lasting change when you are willing to say yes, even if that means you have to do it messy for a while.

The Lord's request for a career change started during a lengthy prayer with my dear friend and spiritual mentor, Stacy McElvaney. She prayed over my gifts and calling, asking for revelation from the Lord about my future. When we finished praying and opened our eyes, Stacy clapped and laughed with excitement and celebration. I was confused. How could she be so excited when my life was a complete mess? She continued smiling and joyfully proclaimed, "God just showed me an image of you standing on stage, holding a sparkly microphone!" I quashed her excitement abruptly with heavy tears. They weren't tears of relief and hope; instead, I collapsed into myself and confessed to her that I had debilitating stage fright and was equally terrified of my own voice. At the time, I was frequently mocked and punished for attempting to stand up for myself as I sought justice for what I had been through. Stacy responded with a warm smile, "That's okay; in Christ, you can do all things" (Philippians 4:13).

In that moment, almost unknowingly, I picked up the Shield of Faith and charged into battle, reclaiming the authority I had so often surrendered to the enemy.

Your Tag Is Showing: Exposed Insecurities and Proving Them Wrong

As you may already know, creating something new, whether it's a business, a platform, a message, or a ministry, will require you to deconstruct parts of your life and career that you've already built. There's no doubt that He will have you climbing mountains and trudging through valleys to achieve your goals, but He will also move you in His timing while He teaches you discernment around your gift and calling.

"I did it; I joined that expensive business group!" I exclaimed. I had discovered the solution to my "Where do I begin?" problem and couldn't wait to tell my friend about my brave decision. I figured it was a worthy investment to join this exclusive group, stacked with accomplished members who had already proven to be successful with their first steps into the business world. In this group, hundreds of people represented all the things I didn't think I would ever be. Though I felt like an imposter among these talented and driven members, I was confident that this would be the place where I would learn the "how-to" steps needed to get started in this mysterious calling that God had set aside for me.

Among the many impressive members, there was a charismatic man who exuded confidence; he appeared to be limited by nothing. He had a large, well-established platform, a podcast, and a coaching program. He was deeply admired by the community for his success and the millions of downloads, views, and followers he had gained. One day, with all the courage I could muster up, I asked him if he would be willing to meet with me and give me some business insight. He laughed in a mocking tone, embarrassing me more than I want to admit, and said, "I charge five hundred dollars for thirty minutes of my time." He then moved swiftly into question mode. In a demanding tone, he asked, "What's the problem?"

His question was simple and not unlike many questions posed by other members who had generously helped guide me, but the authority in his booming voice caused me to explain myself like a child who was falsely accused of talking in class. I spent thirty minutes exposing every single insecurity and limitation I had, including all of the personal circumstances that were crushing me. Through heavy tears and with shame and embarrassment, I further confessed the details of my struggles, which included being frequently objectified by men in both my personal and professional life. He stopped me there and asked more probing questions.

I assumed he was trying to understand what my personal problems had to do with my business. I explained, "When people see what I look like, I get unwanted attention from men and unkind comments from women."

He continued on with more questions, asking, "Why does that bother you?" and "How is that a problem?" I spoke excessively and emotionally, never stopping to recognize the unsafe exposure of my deepest emotional sunburns.

I had spilled over our time answering his continuous questions when, suddenly, he raised his voice sharply and nearly shouted. "You're a hot chick; go be a hot chick!" He then lowered his voice to his normal authoritative tone and said, "Stop fighting what you are, and lean into it; you're making this harder than you need to."

I left that meeting feeling embarrassed, dejected, ashamed, and trapped in an external identity that limited me from connecting with others authentically. This moment left me believing the secular business myth: I'm not cut out for entrepreneurship. I had always been considered "too sensitive," confident about just one thing: I would never, ever have skin thick enough for entrepreneurial success.

Clothed in Determination: Modern-Day Mary Magdalene

Mary Magdalene was a disciple of Jesus and one of the many women who financially supported His growing ministry. She is mentioned several times throughout the four gospels of the New Testament and is most notably recognized for her unwavering faith and loyalty to Jesus and His teachings. But Matthew, Mark, Luke, and John, the authors of the four gospels, fail to mention who Mary was before she met Jesus, only that she was delivered from seven demons, which is undoubtedly a story of true change and healing. It's very clear that who she became, standing witness to the life and work of Jesus and His growing ministry, was far more important than her past and any of the ways she was exploited, abused, belittled, tricked, or naive to the dangers that once threatened her spiritual safety. As my faith has grown and my shield has become more prominent, I often reflect on the journey that led me to this point. I also wonder about Mary and what she may have escaped to become His faithful follower.

It seems I'm not the only one who has a deep curiosity about Mary's story before being healed and led by Jesus. In many instances, Mary Magdalene's story is sensationalized and misrepresented by those who focus on false representations of her character and lurid details of her past rather than the profound significance of her transformation. She has been negatively labeled and her character sharply confined by many who desperately want to fill in the gaps in her story and speculate on the decisions she may have made that led to such a deep struggle.

Strangely enough, I often feel comforted by these narratives about her and divinely strengthened by how I imagine she would react to being negatively labeled by others. I picture her warmly smiling at her accusers as she calmly turns to fix her eyes on Jesus. Her actions are decisive and without emotional reaction as she confidently refocuses on where her true identity lies—in Him.

If you haven't noticed the theme running through my story, I was attracted to abusive rhetoric, often surprisingly motivated by the belittling words spoken over me by people I cared deeply about. I was also willing to give up authority if it meant not upsetting others. I worked so hard to be loved and understood, but my unworthiness continued to grow until I realized that the enemy had gripped the shiniest parts of me, leaving me emotionally, mentally, and physically bankrupt without Jesus.

There were two labels that I began this journey with that triggered ungodly responses in me, including a deep desire for validation from others. These labels were "Gold Digger" and "Daddy's Little Rich Girl." These might have no meaning to you or they may prompt some judgments about me and my story. Still, they represented my deepest emotional sunburns and a multitude of insecurities that the enemy poisoned me with throughout my life, starting as early as six years old when I was introduced to pornography by a beloved family member. This was a shame-filled secret I kept until I was well into my thirties because I had far less credibility than he did. These were labels that the enemy used to keep me from speaking up against the abuse I suffered. Labels that were created by envious people who were threatened by my talents and achievements. Labels that kept me meek, defenseless, limited, and silent.

I've always had difficulty telling my story because there's typically a lack of curiosity about the details but an overwhelming desire to label the role I played in my struggle. That stopped when I was blessed to hear Lysa TerKeurst speak. She is the author of many best-selling books about painful, difficult subjects, including *It's Not Supposed to Be This Way*, where she writes about navigating a life that didn't go as planned. She spoke objectively to a group of hope-filled writers with hard stories to share. During her speech, she said, "Privacy is not the same as secrecy." Today, the need to keep secrets for others is gone. Where there was hurt, forgiveness now resides. Where bitterness once thrived, understanding has emerged. Where there was silence, a still, small voice now stands in justice over it all. This voice, a gift from Him, compels me to speak the truth, not out of malice but out of a deep commitment to the healing that only Jesus can bring.

God made you, like me, a victor, not a victim. He rewrites the hardest of stories, teaches you to overcome, and guides you to rebuild again and again until you get it right. What if you're just a modern-day Mary, letting go of your current struggles to walk obediently and confidently in Him?

What Are You Wearing: Negative Beliefs

Ding! The elevator door pinged loudly as it reached the executive floor of one of the largest corporate campuses in the United States. The fancy doors opened with the same authority as the charismatic executives getting off the elevator who had privileged access to this coveted floor. This was the moment when the Lord met me to confirm my friend Stacy's vision, His invitation to stand on stage and hold a sparkly microphone.

> "God made you, like me, a victor, not a victim. He rewrites the hardest of stories, teaches you to overcome, and guides you to rebuild again and again until you get it right."

Keep in mind that, at that time, I was "just" a single mom, working in a family business while struggling to see a way out of my circumstances. Just months after Stacy and I prayed together, I moved my office into a shared space that was leased by my company. There, I met two executive coaches who specialized in leadership development and corporate training: Ed Beard and Janet McCracken. They were my landlords but quickly became my mentors as they began to believe in me and my potential. They plucked me out of my daily life and invited me to attend training events and coaching sessions. During one of those special invitations, they invited me to Los Angeles to help facilitate a training event for the vice presidents of a well-known Fortune 500 company, a longtime client of theirs. I happily accepted their invitation and arrived in California with a business suit and the idea that I must be on the right track with what God had revealed. This sure felt like a stage and a sparkly microphone. . . .

I badged through security and was being escorted to the executive elevator when I suddenly felt a wave of insecurity wash over me. I noticed how people were looking at me, and it was clear they assumed I was important. But it came with some confusion, which I assumed was rooted in the fact that I really didn't belong there. Moments after entering the executive elevator, I noticed an itchy, scratchy, uncomfortable clothing tag that had warped into a weapon at my neck, following the washing of my suit jacket. As I tried to hide behind the false confidence I had dressed in that morning, the tag was positioned in a way that caused distraction and continuous irritation for the duration of the day.

That tag and the discomfort that ensued created a whirlwind of internal self-doubt. During the short elevator ride, while smiling confidently on the outside, I internally broadcasted these messages to myself: "You're too young." "They're going to laugh you out of the room." "You're not smart." "You don't belong here." "You're not important." "You're just a pretty face." "Nobody respects you."

The number of negatives I rolled around and repeated to myself seemed endless, and it was then that I realized, in the wake of escaping an abusive relationship, I had become my own bully. This was the moment when I recognized that all of these negative beliefs were also negative labels. Labels I was willingly wearing and desperately trying to tuck in and hide. Labels that spoke of what I had been through and what I had learned to believe about myself.

In 2020, I started tearing off these negative tags, similar to the retail tag you rip off when you buy a new outfit. I figured that, if I wasn't willing to wear it fashionably on the outside of my clothes, it was certainly a label that needed to be removed, redefined, or reworded as I considered the truth of my godly identity. That was my message, my mission, and where I found the Lord's healing. It involved writing the negative labels that were holding me back on blank tags and attaching them to the outside of whatever I happened to be wearing that day, which in most cases was a T-shirt that read "Prove them wrong." I then challenged myself to redefine my life, work, and identity as I faced my fears, insecurities, and the emotionally abusive words spoken over me in my past.

I hope you're not currently experiencing negative or limiting beliefs along your entrepreneurial journey, but I believe most of us run into similar emotional blocks when we're navigating our lives *and* an additional business plan crafted by the Lord. If you bump into the myth, "I'm not cut out for entrepreneurship," I challenge you to listen closely to the message of internal self-doubt and try to label it. Then imagine wearing that label on the outside of your clothing, letting the people you associate with see it, read it, and make assumptions about it. You'll learn that you may also be a modern-day Mary, letting go of the past as you step forward to become who He says you are.

These are just some of the negative labels I've intentionally removed up to this point: #stupid, #crybaby, #failure, #weak, #ornamental, #naive, #immature, #irrelevant, #broken, and #worthless. And though there are stories behind each of these emotional sunburns, the details matter less than who I've become on the road to godly freedom. I now consider myself #wise, #patient, #forgiving, #understanding, #resilient, #brave, #thoughtful, #unafraid, #capable, and #coachable, among many others.

You see, removing negative labels that hold you back will create space for positive identifiers that appropriately describe who you really are and who you are still becoming. But if you find yourself believing the lie that you aren't cut out for entrepreneurship or the big call over your life, I invite you to download my free *Burden to Blessing* workbook. It will help you reframe your big struggle and realize the abundance of opportunity within you that is waiting to be explored, expanded, and shared with others.

 THE TRUTH

"God has given you everything you need, and He will grow you where you're feeling underdeveloped."

"FOR WE ARE GLAD WHEN WE ARE WEAK AND YOU ARE STRONG. YOUR RESTORATION IS WHAT WE PRAY FOR"

(2 Corinthians 13:9, ESV).

MEET BEE ANDREEN

About the Contributor

MEET BEE ANDREEN, an integrative business coach and Certified Master Splankna practitioner who has partnered with God to transform her insecurity and complex self-doubt into a wellspring of courageous confidence. After achieving financial freedom through multiple business ventures, Bee now dedicates her life to helping others overcome emotional blocks and rebuild through hardship.

As a multi-skilled entrepreneur, speaker, coach, author, podcaster, and the founder of Embolden Label, a mentorship community for highly sensitive entrepreneurs, Bee is a beacon of inspiration as she helps her clients remove the negative labels holding them back from godly freedom and sustenance.

2

Use What You Got

By Tamra Andress

The Lie
"Money Is Evil"

I opened my Bible (feeling vulnerable as I prepared to minister for the first time) in front of a room full of women who I had invited a couple of days before through a mysterious text message. It read something along these lines: "Join me at the start of the new year to go on an adventure of growth together. I see you, and I'm calling you higher." This experience was painted as one that would reignite passions within us, connect us to the core of who we are, and get us dreaming bigger than we currently were, about a life we didn't have to wait until "one day" to live—specifically focused around the concept of our profession. Proverbs 31 was my landing place. I read the epilogue titled "The Wife of Noble Character," verses 10–31. (I'd encourage you to do the same and not just pick out the most famously recited verses; there's rich stuff to be found.)

After a decade of entrepreneurship without Jesus at the helm, I knew this next endeavor would be wildly different. I wanted to be a wife of noble character. I wanted to provide for family and friends and the community. I wanted to work with eager hands, no matter what time of day, what hat I was wearing, or who I was helping. I didn't want to focus on the one thing I was good at or had been recognized for or paid for in the past.

I wanted to combine a multitude of talents and knowledge points to do something . . . anything . . . different. I was standing up against the status quo of limiting my passions to a nine-to-five, against making it common practice to hone in on only one facet of self (though I had always been an entrepreneur), and against just "picking my niche," which limited my whole self from showing up—that's another lie we'll save for another chapter. Instead, I was ready to express myself just like the wife of noble character—fully. She was a cook and a seamstress, an investor and a farmer. She was a tradesperson and a businesswoman. And she was not ashamed of it. In fact, even her husband was respected because of her diligence.

So there I was, presenting this grand affair to these ladies. Knowing with certainty that God was calling me to this. I asked them to raise their hand if this woman sounded like someone they'd want to become, and the entire room eagerly raised their hands. And so I made my first offer, without having any idea what I was actually doing. At this point, I did not know the intricacies of a pitch or a CTA (call to action). I was fairly aloof to long-term investment planning, budgeting, or systems, and I never considered all the resources it would take to manage a program or a community. I didn't know business consulting like this was even a "thing" or that I was stepping into the world of coaching at large. None of this had ever been exampled to me. I wasn't overly active on social media yet, so I hadn't been tagged or targeted by the algorithm or big-name players at large or with content specific to the industry.

God said, "Do this," and I simply jumped all in, like any puddle-jumping, mud-pie-making schoolgirl would. At that moment, I hadn't spent a penny on branding, web development, social media, resources, etc. I was just being obedient.

The investment to get started was a whopping $37 a month. We easily spend more on lattes each week, but I had conjured up in my mind that this was all they could afford, and if I charged money for this business model (though I believed it was ministry), I was bad because money was bad. In addition, valuation wasn't a conversation in my head about this type of business building, let alone the idea of marketplace ministry. And, although I had been an entrepreneur for a decade at that point in my life, retail sales, personal training, and product development felt very different from this mystical idea of building a movement with God.

It wasn't until nearly a year in that the dollar signs started to not make sense, and my energy investment started to feel lackluster alongside a growing awareness of the idea of ROI (return on investment). "Just do what makes you happy" felt like a great idea initially . . . but when there are uncommunicated expectations (like financial needs), we can allow resentment to grow in our hearts. What had changed from a year before when $37 felt like a safe number?

The industry calls it "comparables"—*know your comps*. What is the person who is marketing a similar service charging, and where do you measure up? As you may already be sensing in your spirit, this alone can be a trap. First, you're being asked to "compare yourself," but you've heard time and time again that "comparison is the thief of joy." You are also being pressured to place a sticker on something, a sticker that does not take into account the historical knowledge involved or the investment assessment you generated to place yourself in this arena. You're not speaking to the full understanding of the value exchange between you and the client. Insert imposter syndrome. It's a slippery slope.

Referring back to the latte-consumption ladder—how did we go from a $3 coffee to an $11 latte in a couple of years? COGS (cost of goods sold) comes into play—inflation, wages, the list goes on. I don't want to lose you here talking about all this business jargon because where I want you to land is on the money story evolving in me at that moment and how it relates to your entrepreneurial path.

There are so many lies compounded in our money stories. We price and sell out of our own bank accounts, which can inhibit our understanding of value. And, often, if the thing we are selling has to do with ourselves, our money mindset can link to generational bondage from belief systems we had no control over. What limiting beliefs did you inherit, or perhaps, what gifted resources were you entrusted with? Regardless, they can both be to our demise if there is no education behind the financial leverage points needed to thrive.

For as long as I can remember, I knew the rule of tithing 10 percent, but even within the Church (an institution designed to equip and establish disciple makers), the topic of money is often skirted around. And as long as you give your monthly allotment, you're good. It's even been misunderstood, out of context of course, that having a lot of money—being rich—is bad. (This is very generalized, so please hear my heart and catch the point.) Stories of the rich young ruler and the camel passing through the eye of a needle swirled in my mind. Money can easily become an idol if it's our focus, and yet, it can be critical to attain. Our eyes can fix on the wrong things, and we can end up conceding to whatever means possible to attain something with finite use instead of our infinite worth in Him.

We can then add the other layer of the persona instilled at a young age: be a good girl or a good boy—share. We want to be "good," so we become generous. We think first about giving and serving more than we do about asking and receiving—which is beautiful—but the problem is we often stop after serving before we ever get to ask or receive. But how can I help others effectively if I don't see my trading as profitable (Proverbs 31:18)?

I started to find deep-seated beliefs in the transformation I was helping others achieve. My membership turned into a one-on-one coaching program—and in less than two years, the $37 a month turned into $3,000 for ten sessions. It then blossomed into a group coaching experience and, later, a $25,000 mastermind. It was not easy, but once I invested in myself, I realized my value in an entirely new way.

What you see missing in the market on your personal journey is likely God's way of revealing that you're meant to fill it.

I finally understood what it meant to "pay to play." I felt clear on the process of investing, i.e., giving, to receive. The more I did this, the more I was able to not only enjoy the process of helping others achieve their version of the Proverbs 31 lifestyle but also see men and women flourishing in the wholeness of who they were called to be. The market that the Proverbs 31 woman traded in was just like this new-age, digital marketplace, where we now operate. But I soon hit another ceiling in the process.

> "What you see missing in the market on your personal journey is likely God's way of revealing that you're meant to fill it."

What is the longevity of a "passion project" if it's not being fueled by something other than just me? The answer God revealed to me wasn't about how much more I could make. It was how much more I could earn to help serve more people, which took more people—not shocking since He is always advocating for the body at large, not just the one. Even though He leaves the ninety-nine for the one (Matthew 18:12), He still brings them back to the collective whole. We are meant to do things in community! So hiring became an emphasis. I imagined the Proverbs 31 woman had help, from volunteers to family and community members and perhaps even servants or paid employees. Regardless, an ecosystem like she built isn't achieved single-handedly, even though our limited lens might lead us to believe otherwise. So there I was, building year by year and inviting new people into the mission who felt aligned to the call and served within their unique gifts . . . and God said, "Don't take a penny."

Wait, what? You've got to be kidding me! I've been grinding (this was pre-rhythms-of-grace-practicing Tamra, of course). We're turning six figures, and I can't touch it? Now, in His defense (not that God needs me to defend Him), this wasn't a new call or mandate. To this point, years in, I hadn't taken one penny from the business. I had promised myself this would be self-funded. We started with zero dollars, and I wanted to be focused on passion, service, and growth. With my history in the entrepreneurial hustle, I didn't want to lose my sense of self to the world ever again. The Lord had captured my heart, and it was my mission to remain faithful to what He was inviting me into while also generating momentum, which requires investment. And, perhaps, in the back of my mind, "Money is evil" crept around, taunting me. So even though "Don't take a penny" was new language for this milestone income our company had generated, it was not too shocking. More so, it was a tip of the hat. Thanks, Papa God, for I can keep going. And I did. I kept building and grinding, but my auto-pilot, pre-learned tendencies of control and people-pleasing would lead to confusion and isolation in the journey. Yet, He would lead me back to that moment of worship where He said, "I am enough. You don't need more of anything besides me." Gosh, that rings true for us all. I even coauthored another book called *More Than Enough: The Silent Struggle of a Woman's Identity*, where we unpack this truth deeply because it's so vitally important to our purpose.

Oddly, when I heard His whisper again, I felt utter peace, even though it made absolutely no sense in my mind or to my comfort or ego . . . but it didn't matter. I had peace from the Lord to let me go on for another year not pouring into our home-front responsibilities—something that, truthfully, didn't make sense. I understand this doesn't pertain to everyone, and hopefully, these won't be the words He speaks to you too. But it does have rich significance for you because I'm almost certain God will, or perhaps already has, asked you to do something really big, beyond yourself, while risking it all for "nothing." And yet, in hindsight, you will have gained so much more in the process. A pastor once said, "You can't take a hearse to heaven," and doesn't that ring true? The treasures stored, the crowns given, the eternal glory, those are worth it to me.

So how do you move past the money blocks, the poverty mentality, the cultural norm of greed, the rat race of just scraping by, the one-man-show season, and perhaps the no-personal-profiting plan to remain in peace for what's ahead? Let's explore this foundational building scenario and how it may parallel your infrastructure, dually related to finances through the lens of Solomon. Get your Bibles and business plans out now, and let's begin.

In 1 Kings and 2 Chronicles, we read about Solomon (David's son) and when he was anointed as king. Upon his first encounter with the Lord, he requested a profound "resource" of wisdom rather than riches, and God was pleased and gave in abundance.

> Do you recall when God anointed you—when He perhaps changed your name and set you at the right hand of the Father to rule and reign with Him (Ephesians 2:6)? Technically, this was your salvation moment, the moment when you became a son or daughter, which also made you a king or queen and coheir with Christ (Romans 8:14–17). How have you requested He supply your needs? Have you asked for wisdom or riches?

Upon his anointing, Solomon was given an inheritance from his father who had amassed a large amount of wealth during his reign (from wars, plundering, and gifts). He was also given a vision and a plan of precision connected to the building of the temple. This was a project David knew, by God's Word, he would not be able to bring to fruition as a "man of war" (1 Chronicles 28:3). Instead, his son would take the throne as the director and builder of the temple that would glorify God.

> You have been given an inheritance from Christ himself with predestined purpose and good works that will honor and glorify God. And even more, it is a promise secured by the Holy Spirit. Unlike the feeble ways that we can squander inheritance here on Earth, this is a guarantee. But if you go deeper into other translations and contextual verses, you discover it's doubly understood that we are God's inheritance, according to His will for us as children adopted into His family. So it's less about "What's in it for me," like a fat check being stroked, and more about what's in it for Him—that's where the glory part comes into play (Ephesians 1:11–14). We also have to consider the generational past, given to us in the context of

finances, belief systems, mindsets, our bodies, etc. I don't want to get into a DNA vs. epigenetics convo here, but I do want you to recognize soul ties and bondage points. Solomon appeared to step into a pretty sweet deal in becoming king after his father who had glorified God. But may we not forget the adultery and sibling debauchery that occurred for Solomon to get there. Everyone has a story, and spending time holding space for it to be faced so you can shift, become, and be free is critical.

I Kings and 2 Chronicles continue into the building phase of the temple Solomon is famously known for. One of his first endeavors was re-establishing relationships that would be valuable to the resource needs of the construction blueprint given him. This plan, like any good contracting write-up, included precision and details that allowed for accuracy, accountability, and longevity.

We have been raised in a "me-centric" society that focuses inward and selfishly desires accolades, ultimately eliminating effective growth, firm structure, abundant resources, and supportive efforts. Through the lens of business building and project implementation, we may understand the importance of hiring the experts and resourcing their toolboxes, but what about the helping hands of implementation, community connectivity, and stewardship? Solomon did all of the above, and often, he did it on barter. Mind you, we aren't advocating for slave labor, but volunteers are an integral opportunity for a shared vision to come to fruition. This methodology is rarely utilized as a first choice. Instead, we waste financial resources and go outside of the connective relationships we have been intentionally gifted to serve alongside. Precision in expertise is to be used as needed, of course, but community design can truly turn a mission into a movement.

As Solomon continued the project, we saw him create from a grandiose lens of resources, with symbols and images representing the heart of God in precision and excellence. He was not concerned with the selfish ambition of fame or harboring anything out of greed. Instead, he used the purest gold and the most precious metals to build. Cutting no corners, he finished the project in its entirety. It took him seven years.

Do we limit our understanding of resources based on the world's presentation of having "enough means" and not having "what it takes?" Do we honor God with the branding and images and projection of who He is through our infrastructure (even if digital buildings)? Would people know who our Father is based on our levels of excellence, honor, and stewardship? Can we say we'd be willing to put our hand to this endeavor if we knew it would drain our reserve of cash, potentially risk our relationships, require limitless leadership and intentionality, and, perhaps, last longer than a half-decade before we ever saw our product complete? Do we try to cut corners in hopeful anticipation of finishing early and making it easier on ourselves? I'm saying *we* because I've been tempted all too often by the projected business plans, the get-rich-quick schemes, and the cravings for comfort, but the further I remove myself from the Ponzi schemes and run to the Father's divine plans, I'm gifted exquisite blueprints, just like Solomon. Our role is follow-through. The fruit of self-control will be born from our obedience as we abide and follow the plans laid before us.

In the final stage of construction, Solomon ordered the ark be brought back to the temple while the priests raised their trumpets, cymbals, and voices, blessing and praising the Lord. And Solomon dedicated the house of the Lord, offering sacrifices, gathering the people for prayer and supplication, memorializing the moment, celebrating it through consecration, and bringing together those of the cities to glorify God who had kept His promises to His plans and His people.

Honoring happens throughout the entire process, and celebration is the totality of the acts of worship day by day and year by year. It invites others into the experience and commemoration of what has happened. When was the last time you celebrated with your family, your team, or your community about the system you built or how far you have come? Have you consecrated your build to the Lord?

After the festivals ceased and everyone went home—at that moment of achievement and completion of the plans—the Lord revealed himself again to Solomon. He spoke "if/then" statements about his faithful integrity, uprightness, and worship posture.

> The Lord is a promise-keeper and asks us to remain in the promise with Him—we do have free will after all. He wants to be in an intimate relationship with us, and His inheritance and blessings don't stop upon completion of a project but remain as we pursue Him faithfully and in purity. It is not by our works that He loves us, but He does have standards.

After this work was completed, we were told that there were more projects, more power struggles, more pleasures, and more prosperity—even though we know that Solomon's will didn't always align with the will of God. But for the sake of extracting the wisdom within his implementation of the temple project and his overall reign as king, we will land on what he did well so that we may not only start well but finish well too.

So here's the intersection of Solomon, the Proverbs 31 woman, and us. It's not a lack of diligence. It's not a lack of obedience. It's a fixed focus on the peace that propels prosperity.

It's wisdom that far outweighs the schemes of the world. You may think like I did, that "making money is hard," when, in fact, it's fairly easy

"It's a fixed focus on the peace that propels prosperity."

because you've remained faithful to His plans. You become a magnet for favor because favor follows friction, and you're willing to go first. Gold was in the garden, and it was said by God to be good. So don't let yourself be tainted by false doctrine or a false sense of security. I get it, you may not have carts of bronze or gold rolling to your front doors to build with or a vineyard that you've bought with your earnings. (I don't yet, considering the longevity of this don't-take-a-penny thing. Watch out for my next book! I'm going deep into the "Profit Last" methodology that has been the catalyst to this movement, even this publishing house.) But guess what you do have?

You have an abundance of resources in your hands.

You have time, talent, treasure, and a testimony. You have expertise, excellence, willful efforts, and energy. You have a legacy that's being built as you serve, share, shine, and support out of your many potentials and passions. You are far richer than you think. And the Shoes of Peace are your assured mode of transportation from one endeavor to the next. Just as Jesus sent His disciples two by two, asking them to bring nothing, they were quickly reminded upon their arrival in the cities that their abundance existed through their service to others and the generosity of the whole. With blind faith, they had peace because He had peace. They did take their shoes, by the way. And money was among some of the resources that were provided to them. Money is mentioned in the Bible more than 2,300 times; that's more than twice as much as faith and prayer combined. God is fully aware of our economy, but remember, He operates in His Kingdom economy, not the American dollar.

You may think this doesn't help you grow a profitable business from the bottom line. But what if it did? What if your feet, "Fitted with the readiness that comes from the gospel of peace" (Ephesians 6:15), knew exactly where to take you because God was your CEO and not you? And you went a step further and really believed what He promised— plans to prosper you and not to harm you, plans filled with hope and a future (Jeremiah 29:11). And you stopped hesitating on the mission. And you started to walk into the resources He prepared for you in advance.

Peace is defined as tranquility, freedom from disturbance, or an end to hostilities or war. Your generational ties or your infused and crooked beliefs of faulty money mindsets can rage a war on your emotions, your mind, your body, your faith, and your business. Don't let greed or gullies keep you from moving mountains or building temples. May it all honor God, and may we all get to celebrate what He's done through your surrender. My prayer is that, like Solomon, you have vats full and a generous spirit to fund the projects of heaven here on Earth.

 THE TRUTH

"Money is not evil. The love of money is the root of all evil."

"FOR THE LOVE OF MONEY IS A ROOT OF ALL KINDS OF EVILS. IT IS THROUGH THIS CRAVING THAT SOME HAVE WANDERED AWAY FROM THE FAITH AND PIERCED THEMSELVES WITH MANY PANGS"

(1 Timothy 6:10, ESV).

TAMRA ANDRESS

About the Contributor

TAMRA ANDRESS is a seven-time number-one best-selling author (and counting), featured in *Forbes*, *USA Today*, and many other well-known publications. She's a keynote speaker and top podcaster with *The Messenger Movement*, *Girl's Gone Holy*, and *The Founder Collective*. She's a serial entrepreneur who works with high-capacity Christian leaders, mobilizing them to become millionaire messengers and share the Good News. She is wildly in love with words and the Word! Through her publishing company, F.I.T. in Faith Press, she catalyzes messengers in the marketplace by building business as a ministry, through publishing, podcasting, and platform development while keeping play at the core! Her nonprofit, The Founder Collective, focuses on ordaining and sustaining marketplace ministers through weekly discipleship and The Founder Academy. Her most treasured roles are as a daughter of the King, wife, and mama.

3

Need for Control

By Christina Blincoe

The Lie
"You Are in Control of Your Life"

The world tells us that our success in life is directly related to the hard work, grit, and dedication we put in. We are told to control our lives and the resulting outcomes. But what would happen if we *let go* of our "need for control" and *let go* of our grip? Would everything fall apart, or would God teach us how to lean on what He called us to be?

> **"The world tells us that our success in life is directly related to the hard work, grit, and dedication we put in."**

Welcome to the "Business and Faith Playbook" for *joy-full entrepreneurs*, thought leaders, and faith-filled messengers. Are you tired of doing it your way? Are you ready to change the way you approach business and learn how God can help develop the gifts He has given you?

Thank you for taking the first step by being here and reading these words. You are on your way to unlocking a new level of joy and stillness as an entrepreneur while also learning about the promises given to each of us by our heavenly Father.

Hello, my name is Chrissy, a childhood nickname I reclaimed to be transformed with a childlike curiosity—one without fear. I am so excited to be here! In God's perfect timing, I am in a place to share with you a little about my journey and to give you helpful and practical ways to start walking this out in your life. Trust me; it is never too late. I am praying for you, my friend. Let's get started.

"BE STRONG AND COURAGEOUS. DO NOT BE AFRAID; DO NOT BE DISCOURAGED, FOR THE LORD YOUR GOD WILL BE WITH YOU WHEREVER YOU GO"

(Joshua 1:9, NIV).

God Had Other Plans

I want to take you on a little road trip through my life—the short version. You can read more of my story in my solo book, coming soon.

I was born in Charlottesville, Virginia, and my childhood was marked by constant movement. My family moved a staggering fourteen times before I was in junior high school. Each move happened for the same reasons: we never owned anything, and times were tough. From living in a tent to staying in rental homes or trailers, we never lived in one place for long, and each new address brought a set of challenges, including adjusting to new schools and making new friends in unfamiliar neighborhoods. But through it all, my family stayed together, relying on each other for support and demonstrating resilience in the face of adversity.

When I was five years old, my mom married my stepdad. Unfortunately, our circumstances did not improve. My parents verbally fought all the time. They never seemed to see eye to eye on anything because of the financial stress. Eventually, my family found a home in Park City, Kansas, where we lived during my later school years, but I never felt totally secure. Money was scarce, and we barely had enough food, even though my parents both worked tirelessly just to make it paycheck to paycheck. I longed for stability in my life, but it always felt like the bottom was going to fall out . . . and then it did. During my sophomore year of high school, my mom and stepdad went through a divorce.

I had multiple jobs as a teenager while juggling school, sports, and church activities. Some of these included babysitting for multiple families, bagging ice at the local grocery store, and working in a bakery. You could say this is where I learned how to be an entrepreneur. I realized that if I wanted something, I needed to work hard, but I also realized that I could relate and encourage others positively. I really believe this is where I learned that I had something, deep down, driving me to create a better life for my future family. And though I dreamed of a better life, a true entrepreneur cannot just have a desire or an idea. She must act on the idea, believe in that idea, and share it with others to help her have a better life as well. During these difficult years, I kept prayer journals, begging God to protect me, to keep me secure, and to provide.

There were no family members or friends who could serve as positive and successful role models for me to become a *joy-full entrepreneur*, so I leaned into God's strength. I was the first in my family to graduate college with an international business and accounting degree. Later, my mom, my brother, and my two adult sons all went on to finish their college degrees in fields they were passionate about, and my sister is a very successful real estate professional. So despite the instability and uncertainty that defined my early years, those experiences taught me valuable lessons about perseverance, resourcefulness, and the importance of family. It laid the foundation for the journey that would ultimately shape who I am today as an entrepreneur and a woman of faith.

I was married at age twenty, graduated from college at twenty-two, and soon after, had my first son. Five years later, my second son was born. By that time, however, my marriage was struggling, and though I longed to keep my family together and change the situation, it was one of the darkest times in my life. I was spiraling emotionally, with no control over the circumstances around me, and I wanted to end my life . . . but God had other plans.

After my divorce, I remember sitting on the edge of my bed, crying out to God to take the pain and to help me heal, to help me find a man who would love me and my boys with the kind of love that He wanted me to experience. I begged Him not to put me through the dating ordeal, and I remember praying that if God didn't drop the man at my front door, I planned to raise my boys alone.

That was the moment I saw Jesus, and He said to follow Him, to truly trust Him, and to not let go of His promises. I have not shared this story with many people until now because I know how it sounds, but my relationship with Him throughout my younger years was so close that I really felt Him with me that day, reaching out His hand.

Battling the Need for Control

The need for control in my life comes primarily from two things: fear and pride. I am the oldest child and have a Type A personality. The pressure I felt as the oldest to meet the high expectations I placed on myself and the stress of feeling like I had to be the perfect role model for the rest of my siblings were compounded by the lack of control in my life. I had feelings of insecurity, the pain of divorce, the inability to rely on and trust others, and the isolation I experienced in the corporate world. The result has been a life of holding on with a very tight grip, but I longed to provide more financial security for my kids and create a legacy of hope and faith for them.

And guess what? God did reach out His hand, and in His timing, He provided me with a loving man. And do you know where God placed this man in my life, so I might meet him? Church. My pastor played matchmaker and knew the two of us would be a great couple. It may not have been on my doorstep, but I would say it was close. Joe and I had a son a few years after we married, and Joe blessed our family by adopting my two older sons as his own. My husband's parents eventually came to live with us. We wanted to have grandparents close to our children in a loving, Christian home, and this move blessed us and allowed them to heal from health and financial issues. I had never really experienced this kind of love, forgiveness, and healing in my life, except with my mom and my sister.

As I began to trust God's provision for our lives and what we could do as a family, Joe was struggling in the corporate world. He did not experience loyalty from his employers and was laid off twice, *but God* answered my prayers and blessed our family with a lavender farm business that Joe and I could run together. We still have the business today and run it parallel to our full-time jobs. Joe works for our church, and I continue to work in engineering. When do entrepreneurs sleep? We don't!

Joe and I believe in our business so much that we invest not only our time but our financial backing. We do this because we feel it's important not to go into debt. We have been patient and trusting God in every step and have learned it's okay not to have all the answers. The Lord has shown me over and over in my life that He is not only there, but in His timing, my prayers will be answered. There have been times when what I prayed for was small, but God multiplied my prayer into something I could never have imagined.

"TRUST IN THE LORD WITH ALL YOUR HEART, AND DO NOT LEAN ON YOUR OWN UNDERSTANDING. IN ALL YOUR WAYS ACKNOWLEDGE HIM, AND HE WILL MAKE STRAIGHT YOUR PATH"
(Proverbs 3:5–6, ESV).

The key word in this verse is *trust*. Ask yourself if you are trusting Him with the big dreams you have for your life and your business. Do you believe in your heart that He will expand your life into something much bigger than you can even imagine if you allow Him to and relent to His timing? Remember, we have to be ready to receive His gifts, and sometimes it is in the waiting that we learn to have patience and sit in stillness for what is to come—and learn what He will require from us as we follow His calling for our life.

Our lavender farm and online boutique have grown organically. As the owners, we are the people who greet you at our pop-up shopping events. We are the faces of the company because one of our core values is to connect with others. We do about eighty shows a year, in addition to our full-time careers. Many people ask us how we can grow lavender, work full-time jobs, and do shows on the weekends

> "Ask yourself if you are trusting Him with the big dreams you have for your life and your business."

without falling over, and my answer is always the same. When you are intentional and have a true calling and passion for what you love to do, you get good at time management. We are very fortunate to have the support, love, and help from our in-laws, my mom, and our adult children in different areas of the business.

Over the years, we have done a lot of test marketing to get feedback that helps us grow our product line. We have over forty-five products available for our customers. We also wholesale to other small businesses and white label for companies that want unique branded candles.

One thing I would tell a new or existing business owner is to try things and take risks even if you are only two steps ahead of the competition. One of the areas where we took risks was in the services we provided. As an entrepreneur, you never really know how something will be received until you give it a try. We have had weddings, bachelorette dinner parties, yoga meditation events, farm tours, u-cut lavender experiences, farm-to-table dinners, and picnics in the field. All these services and offerings allowed us to share our home and land with others, and although we had no prior experience, we showed up as ourselves and were widely and well-received. An important lesson we learned was that we needed to develop our niche and nail down our specialty. You really cannot be all things to all people, so do what you love, and cut the rest.

This is true even for the behind-the-scenes work. After several years in business, we hired an accountant, a web designer, a marketing specialist, and a content writer and relied on many inexpensive software tools to help with the rest of the not-so-fun duties of running a business. One of the most important pieces of advice I give anyone in business is to connect with a community of like-minded people. That is what led me to contribute to this powerful anthology for entrepreneurs. Being a part of a community is a great opportunity to get plugged in and start seeing where God will lead you as a like-minded business and faith entrepreneur. Our biggest reward, however, is teaching our children to share their faith, have a growth mindset, go after their dreams, and do what they truly love.

The Armor of God: The Sword

"FINALLY, BE STRONG IN THE LORD AND IN HIS MIGHTY POWER. PUT ON THE FULL ARMOR OF GOD, SO THAT YOU CAN TAKE YOUR STAND AGAINST THE DEVIL'S SCHEMES"

(Ephesians 6:10–11).

"TAKE THE HELMET OF SALVATION AND THE SWORD OF THE SPIRIT, WHICH IS THE WORD OF GOD. AND PRAY IN THE SPIRIT ON ALL OCCASIONS WITH ALL KINDS OF PRAYERS AND REQUESTS. WITH THIS IN MIND, BE ALERT AND ALWAYS KEEP ON PRAYING FOR ALL THE LORD'S PEOPLE"

(Ephesians 6:17–18).

It is not always easy to take up our swords and fight against the enemy. We are not called to do this by *our own strength* but in *His strength*. When we face challenges in life, and we all will, we can find peace knowing God is on our side. "What, then, shall we say in response to these things? If God is for us, who can be against us?" (Romans 8:31). Our armor is the Sword of the Spirit (the Bible), which will help us trust in His living Word and apply it in our lives.

At first, *my strength* was my sword against life's storms. I relied on my ability to follow a career that would support my family. I held on tightly, convinced that my resilience and drive were enough to weather any challenge. Then came moments, many moments (that I will unpack in my soon-to-be-released book), when my grip faltered, and the weight of the world felt too heavy to bear alone. In those moments of vulnerability, I found a new kind of strength—not in holding tighter but in letting go of the illusion of control and the belief that I could navigate every obstacle on my own. It was a humbling realization and one that led me to open my heart to something greater than myself. In surrendering, I discovered a profound sense of peace, knowing that I am held by a power beyond my own. It's a journey of trust and a choice every day as I learn how to lean on *God's strength* when mine falters and find grace in the release. The Bible advises against trying to control everything in your life and encourages us to trust in God's plan and His timing.

I admire and relate most in my life to Peter (called Simon at birth). He was a disciple of Jesus and a fisherman from the Sea of Galilee in Israel. The more I study the life of Peter, the more I see similar traits in my own life. He was a strong-willed person who sometimes acted first before thinking. Can you relate? During one of Simon's first meetings with Jesus, he was given a new name, and his life would be changed. Jesus named him Peter, which means "rock," stable, strong, and secure. It is a rescue story—like mine. Jesus taught Peter what it meant to follow Him and to be the person Jesus called him to be.

A Song of Strength

The song "Strong," by Anne Wilson, is a beautiful reminder of God's promises. It talks about a full surrender to Jesus. We cannot rely on our own strength but in the one who makes us strong. I know I have prayed this many times and love hearing this song, as it is a sweet reminder of *who* gives me strength.

Why has this been a challenge for me, and why do I continue to fall? I am action-oriented and a very driven-for-results type of person. This means I can get in my own way when I try to do things my way. But when we allow God to enter our lives, He is the same yesterday, today, and tomorrow. He is our Creator, the Almighty, our Healer, and the Promise Keeper. God is calling you to have a relationship with Him so He can start to do the work that He has called you to for such a time as this.

It took courage to write this chapter and share the love God has for me. Learning to release all that has held me back allows me to see the life He wants for me. It's time right now for all of us to take our lives back from temptation, corruption, hurt, and pain—and not allow our selfish ways to consume us. It's time to find the true *joy* He has for us. It's time to be still and experience all He has always wanted for us. Who's ready to let go and truly let God take the reins of their life and business?

My Prayer for Each of You

Father, help us to prepare for any battle we face. Help us to keep our eyes focused on you. As we go through our days, help us *stand strong* and not live in fear of the enemy. Please, Lord, equip us today with the armor of God.

Practical Ways to Apply to Your Life and Business

1. Read the Word of God as your sword, your food, and the water that sustains your life.

2. Pray about all things. Even when you do not think He hears you or cares, He is listening. Be intentional about doing your part to heal.

3. Journal. Write down your thoughts and the steps you need to take to find wholeness.

4. Sing. I love to sing and listen to the words of Christian artists to guide my day.

5. Set quarterly goals. Move your business forward, visualizing it to life.

6. Find community. Connect with people who help you to see how God sees you and share your faith with others, unafraid.

 # THE TRUTH

"As a believer, I hold dear the truth that while we all make choices that shape our lives, the ultimate control rests with God."

"BE STRONG AND COURAGEOUS. DO NOT BE AFRAID; DO NOT BE DISCOURAGED, FOR THE LORD YOUR GOD WILL BE WITH YOU WHEREVER YOU GO"

(Joshua 1:9).

CHRISTINA BLINCOE

About the Contributor

CHRISTINA, A.K.A. "CHRISSY" BLINCOE, is a child of God, chosen by Him and held up by His Grace and love for fifty years. She is a wife to her sweet hubby, Joe, and a momma to three amazing sons, Brandon, Trenton, and Isaac. Joe and Chrissy are active with their church family, where they have dedicated over twenty-four years to serving in various leadership roles. Chrissy gives back her time and heart to others and has a deep desire and drive to leave a legacy for her family.

Chrissy currently works for an employee-owned engineering firm in 2024. Throughout her twenty-eight-year career, she has worked with similar firms, learning what it takes to be an entrepreneur and the mindset and spirit behind it. She has a heart to serve with her gifts in technology and business. Chrissy is a Christian business owner, engineer, speaker, author, mentor, coach, and connector.

She volunteers with young people and women entrepreneurs to share her experience in small business. Along with her Master's Degree in Business Relationship Management, she and her husband are the *joy-full entrepreneurs* behind Sweet Streams Lavender.

Joe and Chrissy started Sweet Streams Lavender farm in 2015, in Kansas, focusing on each other's strengths to utilize their time effectively and create intentional connections with their community. The mission of Sweet Streams Lavender is grounded in faith, values, and love for family, friends, partners, and customers they call "friends." Joe and Chrissy are helping others find the beauty in themselves, and God is not done with them yet.

4

Faith-Filled Foundation

By Victoria Ciresi

The Lie
"If You Build It, They Will Come"

Opening my mailbox on July 17, 2016, I discovered a signed copy of *Game Plan for Life* from Joe Gibbs. What's amazing about the timing of this special gift is that earlier that same day, I had signed a franchise agreement with an organization I felt called to build a business with. I had been on a journey for almost a year regarding the next steps in my career, and the Lord continued to lead me toward this one particular path.

Several months before, Mr. Gibbs, someone I had grown up watching coach the Washington Redskins, walked into Sweet Frog on a Friday evening where my husband, three boys, and I sat enjoying frozen yogurt. I felt so much excitement when I saw him walk in! I had so many fond childhood memories of my family watching him lead the Skins to two Super Bowl championships, and seeing him there that Friday night (which, coincidentally, was the Friday of Super Bowl weekend), I knew I had to say hello! Despite my husband telling me not to bother him, I couldn't help myself. Our entire family was decked out in Carolina Panthers' gear (the home team), and talking football was my "in" to connect with him! He was engaging and kind and shared that he, too, was rooting for the Panthers, which my boys loved to hear. Coach Gibbs asked my husband

and me what we did for a living, and we shared details of our day jobs. But we also shared that God was calling us to pursue business ownership. He took our names and our address, and with that, he grabbed his frozen yogurt and headed out the door.

Five months later, the exact date we became business owners, his book showed up at our door. The beautiful thing about his book is that its focus is on biblical principles that lead to success in key areas of life, one of which is business. Coach Gibbs shares that, as "an average Joe," he wants to ensure the reader understands the most important aspects of living a life of victory. He has worked hard throughout his life, but as it relates to work, he references Colossians 3:23 (ESV) as the key to his success, advising us to work "heartily, as for the Lord and not for men."

In this chapter, we will dive specifically into business ownership, and the myth we will unpack is "If *you* build it, they will come." Whatever you are building—a business, a career, a family, a marriage, a friendship— Psalm 127:1 (NLT) tells us, "Unless the Lord builds [it], the work of the builders is wasted." Following the Lord's playbook for my life has been the best thing I have ever done. It wasn't always the case, especially early in my business journey, but important lessons were learned along the way:

1. Wherever He calls me, I need to make Him the primary builder, surrendering my mission to His mission.
2. Success must be defined from God's view and not man's.
3. Following the playbook truly means fully relying on Him!

Where I Was Called

About a year before meeting Coach Gibbs, I walked into a women-only gym on a Saturday morning, where the sign read, "Fit Community of Moms." I was a mama of three (ages four, two, and one) and was in a season of mental and physical drought. This gym was special. It was filled with like-minded women in a similar season. God not only led me there for my physical and mental health, but He also led me there for relational health and connected me to Ashley, a sister in Christ and now one of my dearest friends.

During one morning workout, there was a large white sign hanging in the back that read, "Now Awarding Franchises." Throughout the entire workout, I heard God's voice saying, "This is your next step." I didn't really know what *franchising* meant and had never been a franchise partner or owned a business, but when God speaks, you lean in. I went home that morning and shared with my husband that God was telling me we needed to open a franchise. After a lot of conversation, individual prayer, and prayer together, we pursued this nudge from the Lord.

During this time, my friendship with Ashley grew. Our families had been "doing life together," and I learned that she also felt this same pull. Even though it wasn't a faith-based organization, we felt called and connected to this brand in a divine way. Our families began praying together, and we decided to move forward in a partnership—but with God first.

We were all new to business ownership and didn't have a solid business playbook to follow, but we knew this was where God wanted us, and we were committed to staying faithful to follow His playbook. The first order of business was to establish our entity. None of us being very creative, we ultimately landed on GAVA (**G**eorge, **A**shley, **V**ictoria, and **A**nthony) Wellness, LLC. The mission statement for our business was "To inspire, empower, and transform lives through faith and fitness." We made it our personal goal to put Jesus first and do nothing out of selfish ambition. We established core values of servant leadership, humility, putting others above ourselves, and seeking Kingdom results.

A few weeks after forming our LLC, some major events occurred that created unrest and skewed our clarity. We let fear creep in, and it almost won . . . but God! A day before our scheduled franchise signing, Ash and I were talking on the phone and agreed we needed to pray. It was important to hear from the Lord, and so we prayed for extreme clarity on whether we should move forward with the signing.

Then I went for a run, a favorite place to seek Him. I had so much clarity, peace, calm, and true conviction that He was in this with us. He reminded me of my season of drought. He had called me to step out in faith and passionately pursue Him while serving others in a business model where I found community. As for Ash, He showed up big for her in her Pinterest feed! When I got back from my run, I had a text message that included a screenshot picture that said, "God is greater than our highs and lows—G > < >," and a follow-up text that read, "Does this not look like our business name—GAVA?!" This was the clarity God knew we needed, and it was a promise that He would be in the business through the highs and the lows. He was our builder, even down to our business name! The very next day, with courage and conviction, we signed a development agreement to open a total of three locations within the next three years; Coach Gibbs's book was in my mailbox that afternoon!

The journey to open our first franchise had begun. I need to share the wonderful benefits of becoming a franchise partner with an organization that has established brand recognition and a proven business model. We were excited about having a framework that included areas we didn't have experience in, such as marketing, commercial real estate, and supply chain. With that being said, a playbook designed by man will only get you so far. We knew that the ultimate playbook was seeking the Lord in the journey and having faith in Him. We prayed constantly about every part of our business—the location, the people we would hire, the joint ventures we would partner with, the time spent in the location, our finances, and our roles as business owners. And to ensure that we were fully aligned with God, we were in the Bible daily, seeking His wisdom. We didn't lose sight of our core value of Kingdom results and waited on Him to move before we moved. There was a lot of hard work, discipline, and dedication required, but we felt fulfilled daily. And despite the challenges we faced, we knew God was in it. We were sharing how He was moving in our lives personally and creating a community within our location in a big way, all of which led to profitability.

I'll Take It from Here

A few months after the first location opened, it was time for us to begin planning the opening of the second location. My husband and I both had jobs outside of our franchise, and our boys were now three, four, and six. We began praying about my role within the business, and in 2018, the Lord gave us clarity that I should step away from my day job and focus solely on the business. This step in our journey created an even larger need to rely on the Lord for this business to provide for our family. It was a big leap of faith. We trusted Him and went full steam ahead into the second location with much more confidence, as we had seen success and had some experience under our belts. We believed that with tools, such as the business framework from the first location; guidance from other business owners, including the franchisor; and increased brand recognition in our territory, it would be much easier to scale and find continued success. And so the myth took hold: "If you build it, they will come."

A few things took root during this season that were not from the Lord. I had a need to control every outcome of the business, and my vision of what success looked like became skewed. As a business owner, I am sure there have been times when you believed you had to do everything in the business for it to be successful. I shared in the book *More Than Enough: The Silent Struggle of a Woman's Identity* that my personality is "very" Type A, and now that this was my sole job, I felt the need to take control of every situation. I found myself no longer driven by faith, and I let fear take root, and in that, I lost sight of God's mission for us. I became primarily motivated by profitability, influence in the community we served, and affirmation from my peers. I remember prioritizing the mission of the business above the mission God had for me and my family. I was afraid of failure in the business, and somewhere along the line, I stopped fully trusting that He was in control. I prioritized relationships with my members above my family, and when I was home, I was not fully present with my husband or children. I was afraid that if I was not in the business all the time, we wouldn't be successful. As a result, I spent a lot of time traveling and was in the business more than I was at home. I quickly became burnt out, completely overwhelmed, and empty.

As business owners who seek Kingdom results, it is important to never lose sight of the Lord and His calling for us and our obedience to Him. In the Bible, King Solomon was known for his wisdom, but he became disobedient to God. During his reign, several significant consequences resulted from his disobedience—idolatry, personal displeasure, unrest, division under his leadership, and strife with multiple adversaries. His disobedience was influenced by his many foreign wives who did not know the Lord. At their prompting, Solomon built places for them to worship their gods. His heart turned away from the Lord, and he began to worship them too. Despite God warning Solomon twice, he did not keep God's commandments. As a result of this disobedience, God declared that the kingdom would be torn from Solomon's lineage and divided into ten tribes. Only one tribe (Judah) would remain under the rule of Solomon's descendants. In addition, Solomon faced various adversaries, raised up by God because of his disobedience. These consequences highlight the repercussions of turning away from God's playbook and the resulting impact on one's legacy and the unity of the heavenly Kingdom.

Reclaiming the Truth

Our first location was solely built by the Lord, and our obedience in faith to Him was evident throughout the early part of our journey. We had so much harmony and were truly following His playbook. Our second location was different. We knew God was in it, but we weren't seeking Him as often and began to live the lie: "If you build it, they will come." I am reminded of the verse Coach Gibbs referenced in *Game Plan for Life*: "Whatever you do, work at it with all your heart, as working for the Lord, not for human masters, since you know that you will receive an inheritance from the Lord as a reward. It is the Lord Christ you are serving" (Colossians 3:23–24). This verse encouraged me to approach our franchises and daily tasks with a renewed mindset of wholeheartedness, viewing my efforts to serve the Lord and not the expectations of a franchise playbook. It reminded me of our core value—Kingdom results.

Earthly playbooks can be helpful, especially in skill sets not yet learned or experienced, but they are limited in scope and will only take you so far. It wasn't up to us to build the business; it was up to us to have a solid, faith-filled foundation for the business that God was building. Ephesians 6:14 (NLT) states, "Stand your ground, putting on the belt of truth," and in our journey, I believe that means following the ultimate playbook that God offers. His playbook is boundless, and although it can be difficult to understand and follow at times, we must have faith and trust in Him during each step of our journey.

> "It wasn't up to us to build the business; it was up to us to have a solid, faith-filled foundation for the business that God was building."

We also found that listening and following His playbook can sometimes be more difficult on the heels of success. But we have come to realize that His outcomes will far surpass any outcomes we could set for ourselves.

Fast-forwarding in the GAVA Wellness journey . . . despite success from the world's view, we felt His calling to sell our franchise locations. We didn't know what the future would hold, but we trusted God in this decision. Years later, we both had an even greater opportunity to impact the Kingdom through this same organization, and this could have only been possible with the Lord directing our steps and us trusting His playbook.

Through my journey, I've continually been reminded of this truth: God's plans will always surpass our plans. The most important thing we can do as entrepreneurs is build our foundation on our faith in God. If we do that, they will come!

> "God's plans will always surpass our plans."

People from all over the world came to see Solomon and what God built because what He builds surpasses human understanding. Stand your ground, and put on the Belt of Truth to remind yourself that, no matter what the world says is success or what playbook you are given, God's view of success for you and His playbook (the Bible) are your weapons to fight! As Psalm 127:1 (NLT) reminds us, "Unless the Lord builds [it], the work of the builders is wasted."

Reflect on Your Foundation

- What is God's mission for my business?
- What does success look like from His view?
- Am I in conversation with Him daily through prayer and reading His playbook, the Bible?

 **THE TRUTH**

"Success in your business starts with a firm foundation of faith and a steadfast pursuit of God."

"STAND YOUR GROUND, PUTTING ON THE BELT OF TRUTH AND THE BODY ARMOR OF GOD'S RIGHTEOUSNESS"

Ephesians 6:14 (NLT).

"UNLESS THE LORD BUILDS A HOUSE, THE WORK OF THE BUILDERS IS WASTED"

Psalm 127:1 (NLT).

VICTORIA CIRESI

About the Contributor

VICTORIA CIRESI, born and raised in Maryland, currently resides in Denver, North Carolina. She is a mother of three boys and a wife of eighteen years. She was raised in a large family of nine children, with two brothers and six sisters. At twenty-two, she dedicated her life to Jesus. She is a best-selling author with a passion for writing and a compassionate dedication to ministry. She runs Casa Gioiosa (Joyful Home), where she serves those in need through prayer and meals. Victoria also works outside the home, serving as an executive leader for a rapidly expanding fitness franchise. She has extensive experience in business management, leadership, and HR and currently leads the people strategy for the organization. With her life experiences, leadership in a women-focused organization, and six sisters, she has a heart for ministering to women so they can find their true identity in Jesus.

5

The Power of the Wills

By April Foster

The Lie
"Willpower Equals Success"

While worshipping, I had a vision. The Father said, "I am the Potter, and you are my clay." He led me to move to the ground on bent knees, where I curled myself into a ball with my face down to the ground. The Lord placed His hands securely around me and encouraged me to move my body as much as possible while remaining in a ball. As my forehead continued touching the ground, darkness surrounded me. My uncomfortable body tried to move, but the position made it difficult.

I cried out in my spirit to Abba God, "I can't move! I feel stuck. I am not free to move."

The Father replied, "I created you to be movable. I formed you when you were born. I molded you and made you perfect. Through sin, you fell and became potsherds, broken and fragmented. I created you to be flexible. Instead, you became formed and broken. But then, when you were reborn, I remade you from all the broken pieces and lovingly put them back together. I didn't put you back together to be immovable. I put you back together to be pliable, four-dimensional, movable."

As I remained in the ball, I felt the spirit of the Potter surround me and apply massive pressure on all sides of my body and the top of my back.

I cried out again to Abba God from my fifty-year-old body, "This is so uncomfortable!"

The Father said, "So start moving. I am giving you the frame."

"Okay! I am going to move!" I said. Timidly, I moved a little.

The Father said more directly, "I want you to move. I am holding you." He repeated, "I am holding you. I want you to move. You are free to move."

I stretched my legs from kneeling to standing, but my upper body remained hanging downward, head and arms dangling toward the ground. The Father was so encouraged and said, "That is good! Keep doing it! Keep moving! Make your way."

I then began grabbing pieces of something from deep within the ground that I saw in the spirit and released them above my head into the air. I heard Abba God continue to encourage me and remind me every time I moved to keep moving. The more I moved, the more room He gave me.

The Father continued to hold me and shape me as I moved. He was so pleased with what was being formed. Before I spoke, He knew what I was thinking. He said, "I know you want to experience freedom, but the freedom you seek can only be found in Me. You were born into the world, and I allowed you to do things your way. I never left you. I let your choices to sin naturally take their course of consequences. You broke. I took your broken pieces and remade you. This time, I want you to experience my freedom in this place where I am actively molding you."

> **"I took your broken pieces and remade you."**

The dimensional depth of beauty—as the Potter continued to shape me as I moved—was overwhelmingly peaceful and joyful. He reminded me I was His art piece that He desired to display to the world!

"FOR WE ARE GOD'S MASTERPIECE. HE HAS CREATED US ANEW IN CHRIST JESUS, SO WE CAN DO THE GOOD THINGS HE PLANNED FOR US LONG AGO"

(Ephesians 2:10, NLT).

This vision wasn't just for me. It is for you too. We are stepping over a threshold. We are being called to step out and posture ourselves in the hands of our loving Father. He is wooing us to come out of the darkness and into the light. Will you be brave enough to break out of the world's mold? God will pick up your broken pieces and form you.

What does this vision have to do with entrepreneurial success? Everything! Our journey on this earth is to shepherd the plans of God. However, looking back on my career ventures, I confess that I wasn't about the Father's business. I was about my business. My success. My willpower to succeed. I believed that if I just had enough willpower, I would succeed. And that I did. I made my plans, and I succeeded in them. I moved out of my single-mother home just shy of eighteen years old. I put myself through college by working three jobs and graduated with honors in psychology in three and half years. I married my high school sweetheart at twenty-one and had two children, a girl and a boy. I worked full-time, achieved a master's degree in counseling, and taught as a college professor at age twenty-five.

Life was lining up perfectly and fitting neatly into my plans. I ran hard and succeeded: ran a business for ten years, ran in ministry for ten years, and ran a homeschool for ten years. I even ran the tightrope of the corporate world for ten years. If you do the math, I should have been tired of running. I was.

I am an expert in "willpower equals success." I have a proven track record. But what happened when my willpower ran out? Anxiety, depression, and thoughts of suicide—the idols of titles, accolades, and success no longer brought me happiness.

"FOR WHAT USE IS IT TO GAIN ALL THE WEALTH AND POWER OF THIS WORLD, WITH EVERYTHING IT COULD OFFER YOU, AT THE COST OF YOUR OWN LIFE?"

(Mark 8:36, TPT).

What does Jesus offer? Simply, to follow Him. How many times in Scripture does He offer this invitation? Seven times in Matthew (4:19, 8:22, 9:9, 10:38, 16:24, 19:21, 19:28), four times in Mark (1:17, 2:14, 8:34, 10:21), four times in Luke (5:27, 9:23, 9:59, 18:22), and seven times in John (1:43, 8:12, 10:27, 12:26, 13:36, 21:19, 21:22). That is a total of twenty-two times that Jesus calls us to follow Him.

Though I believed that I was completely surrendered to Jesus as my Lord and Savior, was I really following Him? Or was I just giving lip service to the Lord? Like Peter, I argued with Jesus after He laid out His plans (Mark 8:32). He invited me to walk away from my plans and shift my willpower to follow Him. I wish I could say I took Him up on His offer the first time. But like the recorded invitations in the Bible, He continued to invite. I didn't count how many times, but I am pretty sure it was more than twenty-two. I wasn't convinced that His plans were better than mine. And like Peter, Jesus reminded me through Scripture saying, "For your heart is not set on God's plan but man's!" (Mark 8:33, TPT).

I came crashing into the truth of the great I AM. In the wisdom of Solomon, there are three Proverbs that should be noted as the Lord softened my heart to follow Him:

"BEFORE YOU DO ANYTHING, PUT YOUR TRUST TOTALLY IN GOD AND NOT IN YOURSELF. THEN EVERY PLAN YOU MAKE WILL SUCCEED"

(Proverbs 16:3, TPT).

"WE CAN MAKE OUR PLANS, BUT THE LORD DETERMINES OUR STEPS"

(Proverbs 16:9, NLT).

"A PERSON MAY HAVE MANY IDEAS CONCERNING GOD'S PLAN FOR HIS LIFE, BUT ONLY THE DESIGNS OF GOD'S PURPOSE WILL SUCCEED IN THE END"

(Proverbs 19:21, TPT).

Did I succeed? Yes. Can God work all things together for good? If I believed in His Word and His promise in Romans 8:28, then my answer was yes. Was I really ready to yield to His invitation and stop with all the lip service?

Oswald Chambers's devotional, *My Utmost for His Highest*, states, "The root of faith is the knowledge of God, and one of the biggest snares is the idea that God is sure to lead us to success." In my entitled mindset, I believed that I deserved to be successful. If I worked hard enough and outperformed the person next to me, I would succeed.

> "If I worked hard enough and outperformed the person next to me, I would succeed."

"SO WHY DO YOU KEEP CALLING ME 'LORD, LORD!' WHEN YOU DON'T DO WHAT I SAY? I WILL SHOW YOU WHAT IT'S LIKE WHEN SOMEONE COMES TO ME, LISTENS TO MY TEACHING, AND THEN FOLLOWS IT. IT IS LIKE A PERSON BUILDING A HOUSE WHO DIGS DEEP AND LAYS THE FOUNDATION ON SOLID ROCK. WHEN THE FLOODWATERS RISE AND BREAK AGAINST THAT HOUSE, IT STANDS

FIRM BECAUSE IT IS WELL BUILT. BUT ANYONE WHO HEARS AND DOESN'T OBEY IS LIKE A PERSON WHO BUILDS A HOUSE RIGHT ON THE GROUND, WITHOUT A FOUNDATION. WHEN THE FLOODS SWEEP DOWN AGAINST THAT HOUSE, IT WILL COLLAPSE INTO A HEAP OF RUINS"

(Luke 6:46–49, NLT).

As an entrepreneur, you must have faith in the success of your business. But was your business built without a foundation? Has your success been solely in your strength?

"UNLESS THE LORD BUILDS A HOUSE, THE WORK OF THE BUILDERS IS WASTED. UNLESS THE LORD PROTECTS A CITY, GUARDING IT WITH SENTRIES WILL DO NO GOOD. IT IS USELESS FOR YOU TO WORK SO HARD FROM EARLY MORNING UNTIL LATE AT NIGHT, ANXIOUSLY WORKING FOR FOOD TO EAT; FOR GOD GIVES REST TO HIS LOVED ONES"

(Psalm 127:1–2, NLT).

Is success an idol for you? Jeremiah warns us about idols.

"THE WHOLE HUMAN RACE IS FOOLISH AND HAS NO KNOWLEDGE! THE CRAFTSMEN ARE DISGRACED BY THE IDOLS THEY MAKE, FOR THEIR CAREFULLY SHAPED WORKS ARE A FRAUD. THESE IDOLS HAVE NO BREATH OR POWER. IDOLS ARE WORTHLESS; THEY ARE RIDICULOUS LIES! ON THE DAY OF RECKONING THEY WILL ALL BE DESTROYED"

(Jeremiah 51:17–18, NLT)

God will bless the *real* you, not the one that performs for a blessing. The performance may bring success, but is it tied to the belief system that you will be blessed? The definition of success becomes skewed. If blessing equals success, then does a curse equal failure? If God always blessed us while in the success mode, it is likely that we would remain there through our willpower. So if we continue to believe the lie that willpower equals success and success equals blessing from God, then the reinforcement to continue to strive for God's favor in our entrepreneurial ventures will be in vain.

"THIS IS WHAT THE LORD SAYS: 'CURSED ARE THOSE WHO PUT THEIR TRUST IN MERE HUMANS, WHO RELY ON HUMAN STRENGTH AND TURN THEIR HEARTS AWAY FROM THE LORD. THEY ARE LIKE STUNTED SHRUBS IN THE DESERT, WITH NO HOPE FOR THE FUTURE. THEY WILL LIVE IN THE BARREN WILDERNESS, IN AN UNINHABITED SALTY LAND. BUT BLESSED ARE THOSE WHO TRUST IN THE LORD AND HAVE MADE THE LORD THEIR HOPE AND CONFIDENCE'"

(Jeremiah 17:5–7, NLT).

Jeremiah continues in verse 9, "The human heart is the most deceitful of all things, and desperately wicked. Who really knows how bad it is?" (Jeremiah 17:9, NLT). How do you know if your motives align with the Father's plans? Be still and ask. Posture yourself at the breast of Jesus, like John, the apostle, and rest your head on the heartbeat of your Lord and Savior. Don't come with an agenda or a laundry list of prayer needs. Just be. Sometimes, we forget that we were created for Him, not Him created for us. In many instances, Jesus went to be alone with His Father. What do you think was happening? Jesus was getting the next plan for His Father's business. If you aren't connecting daily with the Father and His plans, then one day you may wake up and realize your success is just that—your success. Your business can't be sustained in your strength.

"YES, I AM THE VINE; YOU ARE THE BRANCHES. THOSE WHO REMAIN IN ME, AND I IN THEM, WILL PRODUCE MUCH FRUIT. FOR APART FROM ME YOU CAN DO NOTHING"

(John 15:5, NLT).

Don't ask yourself what is happening with your business. Instead, ask what is happening inside you. If what you do is not being filled with unspeakable joy and a peace that surpasses all understanding, then prune it.

Don't be like me and hold on to it, hoping your willpower will change the circumstances. I could feel the tide turn, and what once brought me joy only disappointed me. But instead of choosing to walk away when Jesus called me to follow Him, I just kept pushing. Eventually, it was taken away.

"ANYONE WHO DOES NOT REMAIN IN ME IS THROWN AWAY LIKE A USELESS BRANCH AND WITHERS. SUCH BRANCHES ARE GATHERED INTO A PILE TO BE BURNED"

(John 15:6, NLT).

Fire burns, but fire also purifies! God designed all His children to be in life union with Him.

"BUT IF YOU REMAIN IN ME AND MY WORDS REMAIN IN YOU, YOU MAY ASK FOR ANYTHING YOU WANT, AND IT WILL BE GRANTED!"

(John 15:7, NLT).

When failure finally hit me, the Father had me right where He wanted me. He no longer wanted His daughter to live on a foundation of lies. He told me that setbacks are setups because I was set apart. He loved me too much to allow me to continue on my "success" path.

"I HAVE LOVED YOU EVEN AS THE FATHER HAS LOVED ME. REMAIN IN MY LOVE"

(John 15:9, NLT).

He reminded me, "The world would love you as one of its own if you belonged to it, but you are no longer part of the world. I chose you to come out of the world" (John 15:19, NLT). His plans were never to harm me but to prosper me, protect me, and give me hope and a future (Jeremiah 29:11). His purpose for doing this is clear: "I have told you these things so that you will be filled with my joy. Yes, your joy will overflow!" (John 15:11, NLT).

He asked me to obey His commandments and remain in His love, just as He obeyed the Father's commandments and remained in His love (John 15:10). His commands are defined in John 15:12–13 (TPT): "So this is my command: Love each other deeply, as much as I have loved you. For the greatest love of all is a love that sacrifices all."

Love sacrifices all! Jesus sacrificed His life in hopes that we would sacrifice and surrender our lives to Him. Will you sacrifice your success for a chance to experience a fullness of joy that surpasses all understanding?

The power to succeed comes from aligning your will to God's will. In the death of your dreams, you will discover God's dreams for your life and business. Success is defined as our will falling into the hands of the Almighty Creator of the universe. It is trusting Him every step of the way, but faith is required.

"NOW FAITH BRINGS OUR HOPES INTO REALITY AND BECOMES THE FOUNDATION NEEDED TO ACQUIRE THE THINGS WE LONG FOR. IT IS ALL THE EVIDENCE REQUIRED TO PROVE WHAT IS STILL UNSEEN"

(Hebrews 11:1, TPT).

So hold up your Shield of Faith to protect you from the arrows of doubt! Let faith be your fuel! Remember that the greatest stumbling block of mankind is unbelief. Let the Holy Spirit transform your mind, body, and soul.

"STOP IMITATING THE IDEALS AND OPINIONS OF THE CULTURE AROUND YOU, BUT BE INWARDLY TRANSFORMED BY THE HOLY SPIRIT THROUGH A TOTAL REFORMATION OF HOW YOU THINK. THIS WILL EMPOWER YOU TO DISCERN GOD'S WILL AS YOU LIVE A BEAUTIFUL LIFE, SATISFYING AND PERFECT IN HIS EYES"

(Romans 12:2, TPT).

"EVERYONE WHO HEARS MY TEACHING AND APPLIES IT TO HIS LIFE CAN BE COMPARED TO A WISE MAN WHO BUILT HIS HOUSE ON AN UNSHAKABLE FOUNDATION"

(Matthew 7:24, TPT).

"WHOEVER COMES TO ME, AND HEARS MY SAYINGS AND DOES THEM, I WILL SHOW YOU WHOM HE IS LIKE: HE IS LIKE A MAN BUILDING A HOUSE, WHO DUG DEEP AND LAID THE FOUNDATION ON THE ROCK. AND WHEN THE FLOOD AROSE, THE STREAM BEAT VEHEMENTLY AGAINST THAT HOUSE, AND COULD NOT SHAKE IT, FOR IT WAS FOUNDED ON THE ROCK"

(Luke 6:47–48, NKJV).

A final thought from the wise words of Solomon for building your business:

> ## "WISE PEOPLE ARE BUILDERS—THEY BUILD FAMILIES, BUSINESSES, COMMUNITIES. AND THROUGH INTELLIGENCE AND INSIGHT THEIR ENTERPRISES ARE ESTABLISHED AND ENDURE. BECAUSE OF THEIR SKILLED LEADERSHIP, THE HEARTS OF PEOPLE ARE FILLED WITH THE TREASURES OF WISDOM AND THE PLEASURES OF SPIRITUAL WEALTH. WISDOM CAN MAKE ANYONE INTO A MIGHTY WARRIOR, AND REVELATION-KNOWLEDGE INCREASES STRENGTH. WISE STRATEGY IS NECESSARY TO WAGE WAR, AND WITH MANY ASTUTE ADVISERS YOU'LL SEE THE PATH TO VICTORY MORE CLEARLY"
>
> (Proverbs 24:3–6, TPT).

Let us be wise builders together and build kingdom businesses for the glory of God! Let the Potter mold you as you move freely in truth in His hands!

 **THE TRUTH**

"True success is defined as our will falling into the hands of the Almighty Creator of the universe."

"BEFORE YOU DO ANYTHING, PUT YOUR TRUST TOTALLY IN GOD AND NOT IN YOURSELF. THEN EVERY PLAN YOU MAKE WILL SUCCEED"

Proverbs 16:3 (TPT).

"WE CAN MAKE OUR PLANS, BUT THE LORD DETERMINES OUR STEPS"

Proverbs 16:9 (NLT).

"A PERSON MAY HAVE MANY IDEAS CONCERNING GOD'S PLAN FOR HIS LIFE, BUT ONLY THE DESIGNS OF GOD'S PURPOSE WILL SUCCEED IN THE END"

Proverbs 19:21 (TPT).

"YOU WILL FIND TRUE SUCCESS WHEN YOU FIND ME, FOR I HAVE INSIGHT INTO WISE PLANS THAT ARE DESIGNED JUST FOR YOU. I HOLD IN MY HANDS LIVING-UNDERSTANDING, COURAGE, AND STRENGTH"

Proverbs 8:14 (TPT).

APRIL FOSTER

About the Contributor

APRIL FOSTER, a woman of profound influence, is the daughter of the Most High King, wife to John, and mother of two wildly talented and ambitious adult children. Like her children, she is a go-getter and knows a thing or two about success! She maintains a longstanding business (Fostering Foundations) and currently serves as the area coordinator for T.R.A.C. Life, a national mentoring program for teenagers in foster care. With a heart for homeschooling her children through high school, her passion for pioneering led her to plant Christian classical homeschool communities throughout the southeastern region of Louisiana. She successfully homeschooled her children through high school while equipping and encouraging thousands of others to follow her in this classical movement.

With her undergraduate degree in psychology and master's degree in counseling, she has a mission to rebuild marriages, restore families, and reclaim one's identity in Christ. Her podcast *Bedroom and Bible* undresses the topics where no conversation is off-limits! She is a highly sought trainer and speaker for conferences and retreats, leaving a lasting impact on her audience.

She managed a very successful direct sales business for ten years as a top performer. In addition, she also managed communications in the marketing department for a global homeschool company. She has served in the collegiate realm as a college professor, helping young adults with career planning and life skills. In her earlier years, she was a job coach for developmentally disabled adults. Her contributions extend to being an author in the anthology *Joyous Journey of Loss* and her ongoing work toward publishing her first book in the series *Love Colored the Way*. Additionally, she has published articles and blogs for *Classical Conversations* and *The Old Schoolhouse* magazine.

The mission of her chapter in this *Joy-Full Entrepreneur* anthology is to empower those who struggle with the belief that if you just have enough willpower, you will succeed. The power to succeed comes from aligning your will with God's will. It's in the death of a dream that you discover God's dreams for your life and business.

6

Made for This

By Elisah McGee

The Lie
"You Must Be an Expert"

I slept in my cocoon of blankets, shutting off the pestering thoughts circling down the worn, familiar paths of doubt in my mind. I shut out the deep, muffled voices seeping through the closed door that was reinforced with towels and suitcases, keeping me safely hidden inside. I remained still and silent, careful to sleep perfectly poised so as not to crease my cheeks or curls of short hair. In a deep slumber, I embraced the cover of darkness.

I was afraid . . . afraid of the ribbons of bright colors, patches, and medals emblazoned in my mind despite each man in civilian attire on the other side of the bedroom door. I knew what they were hiding, though—their ranks and histories of success, the wars and scurries they fought in, the dangerous missions accomplished, the depths of their experiences.

Then I was awake, hungry, and wanting to come out of the shadows of my bedroom, but I had to wait. I shrank inward, letting the thoughts continue to circle, taunting, minuscule, dumb, worthless, voiceless.

The steady hum of voices finally shifted to the familiar ebb and flow of friendly banter. I could hear my husband, John. His voice raised high as if retelling a story. Laughter flowed, and I knew it was safe to emerge. Our customers had left.

On cue, I quickly moved the suitcases and towels as if they had never been there to begin with and took a quick look at myself in the mirror, tidying my hair and makeup. I then opened the bedroom door with a confident swing and a full smile. My team greeted me with concern, asking if my head cold had subsided. By this stage in my life, masking issues of anxiety was as easy as emphasizing the effects of a cold, giving me an out if I couldn't quiet the fears. Sure, I didn't feel the best, but I was certainly not on my deathbed and should have been in the meeting.

We were in Las Vegas for the annual SHOT Show, one of our biggest conferences of the year. John and I were in our fourth year of business, and I was CEO. It was 2023, and I still struggled. We had achieved brilliant success, as emphasized by our second year hosting in the uppermost Palazzo Towers. But I still hid in fear at times.

I had stayed at home with my children for most of my adult life and had only achieved the highest position of an executive assistant. I believed the taunting voices in my mind that told me I couldn't hold a conversation. I stumbled over my words. I believed I wasn't well-versed in my industry. I hadn't served in the military, and I didn't know their language of acronyms or which unit was responsible for what. I believed that I didn't meet the expectations of my title . . . but I was tired of the lies swirling in my head and tired of hiding.

Fork in the Road

I finally got fed up with the pestilent thoughts. I kept coming to this fork in the road and choosing the same well-trodden path that was familiar and comfortable—a place where I told myself I couldn't be CEO because I wasn't an expert. The words

"Another moment later, a faint whisper settled on my mind: Maybe you were born for this. I pulled out my Bible to find the verse. I landed in the book of Esther, where a queen was at her own fork in the road"

of motivational speaker Les Brown echoed in my mind: "We came to you, and only you could give us life." It was a speech I had played on repeat, soaking my mind in this idea that talents are born and die with you. Another moment later, a faint whisper settled on my mind: *Maybe you were born for this.* I pulled out my Bible to find the verse. I landed in the book of Esther, where a queen was at her own fork in the road (Esther 4:13–14).

Imagine a newly crowned queen who had hidden her identity from everyone at the command of her adopted father. A queen who was then urged by him to unveil her true identity when doing so would mean certain death.

Queen Esther was confronted by her perfectly kept family secret. Because of a series of events led by the plotting of the king's highest official, Haman, every Jew in all 127 of her provinces was going to be killed. Mordecai, her adopted father, had already freed himself from his silence after hearing the news, publicly mourning at the city's gates for everyone to see that he was Jewish, wearing only a sackcloth and ashes. Esther's secret was still safe. No one knew they were family. Yet, she was overcome with fear. She tried to stop Mordecai, sending clothing to keep him safe from the impending genocide, to keep the secret hidden.

Mordecai refused and told Esther, "Don't think you will escape the fate of all the Jews because you are in the king's palace. If you keep silent at this time, relief and deliverance will come to the Jewish people from another place, but you and your father's family will be destroyed. Who knows, perhaps you have come to your royal position for such a time as this" (Esther 4:13–14, CSB).

It made sense that Mordecai asked Esther to approach the king. She had won the king's version of a modern-day beauty pageant that was held to find a new queen to replace Queen Vashti, who had refused to appear at his feast. Esther was highly favored. "The king loved Esther more than all the other women" (Esther 2:17, CSB). She was perfectly positioned, but she would have to face her fears in order to confront the king. Her fear was real because appearing in court without the king summoning her first typically resulted in death. If Esther somehow survived this step, the next step of revealing her Jewish identity would certainly mean her death.

The Choice

Despite the overwhelming odds, Esther made a bold move. She pivoted from a life obedient to the commands of others, one that was reliant on the comfort her beauty gained. She chose God, putting the fate of her life in His hands. She placed Him at the helm to direct the outcome, regardless of her fear. She led in faith, commanding Mordecai to gather all the Jews in the city together to fast for three days and three nights. She led by example. She fasted and had her servants fast as well. She made a way for God to move.

For years, I was aware of my internal battle, but my weapons for combat were futile. I had to make a dramatic shift. Between SHOT Show 2023 and 2024, I chose the road "less traveled by" as the famous poet Robert Frost described, and it "made all the difference."[2] For me, it was the same road Jesus described—akin to entering the gate of heaven—as "narrow" and "difficult" and found by few (Matthew 7:13–14). I had to follow God. I needed to hear what He thought about me and my position.

> "For years, I was aware of my internal battle, but my weapons for combat were futile."

Helmet of Salvation

Back when we first formed our company, I drew a picture of a woman fully clothed in armor and holding a spear, similar to the goddess I had

2 Frost, Robert, and Louis Untermeyer. 1991. *The Road Not Taken: A Selection of Robert Frost's Poems.* New York: H Holt and Co.

once seen sculpted into a frieze at the Daughters of the American Revolution Museum in Washington, DC. I realized the correlation to Ephesians 6:10–20 as I drew, embracing Paul's teachings of the full armor of God. I had the drawing tattooed on my forearm a couple of years later as a reminder of God's strength in me when armored. As I journeyed forward through bouts of self-doubt, I recognized the power of putting on the Helmet of Salvation daily.

The battlefield in my mind completely shifted when I challenged myself to read the Bible and pray every day, starting in May 2023. I was at a loss, still stuck in the perpetual cycle of thinking I was not a leader in my company. This one simple act created a dramatic shift.

God led me to speakers, such as Simon Sinek, who encouraged me to embrace a different perspective of leadership, one that asserts "there is no such thing as an expert leader," and "we are all students of leadership."[3] This was something I could grab onto. I was an avid student of the defense industry and military. I never gave up learning, gleaning from my veteran fathers, my historian grandfather, my time as a military spouse, and every ounce of my husband's industry knowledge (often to the point of breaking his patience with my poignant and persistent questions). I soaked in rich stories from friends—stories of their experience in military conflicts, time spent in different countries, knowledge of base life, and transitions to industry sales. I sought opportunities to engage and understand the inner workings of the military while also digging into the inner workings of my company.

Then God pushed me into an unexpected adventure. It was a random, sudden call to compete in a national pageant. I answered the call swiftly and was accepted as my state of Virginia's representative. For the better half of a year, I wore a sash and crown in public, spoke at community events, encouraged community members young and old, planned and

3 Sinek, Simon. 2023. "No Such Thing as an 'Expert Leader.'" Filmed at Banca Mediolanum National Convention, in conversation with Stefano Volpato. May 2023. Video, 00:38. *YouTube*, https://www.youtube.com/watch?v=gYNCMX3XxkQ.

hosted an educational fashion show, sang on camera and modeled, created video content, and even accomplished a lifelong dream to write and publish a children's book. This all led up to the culminating national pageant week with me on stage for the first time since childhood to face an audience, my family, my friends, and the judges. I didn't win the crown like Esther, but I gained confidence in each action I took along the way and was outspoken about God's hand in each moment.

God also showed me that I had been doing the work all along in my company. A friend and successful entrepreneur encouraged me a couple of years earlier to "do the work," regardless of what it was I was doing. John and I were at his duck camp base in Utah, philosophizing about business and life with him and his wife into the early hours of the morning. I remember when he sat up in his chair, leaned forward, and told me something that changed my perspective. He said that when he first started his company, he had to do all the jobs, right down to cleaning the toilets and doing the paperwork. He did the work until he hired himself out of it. In one moment, he had completely released me from the shame I felt in the work I was doing up to that point. I considered myself the paper pusher, the admin, the bookkeeper, the one-woman cleaning crew, the inside sales, the purchaser, the HR department, not to mention the wife and the mother. All these things seemed less important than what I considered the most vital task my husband had—producing sales. In just a few words, our friend gave me the courage to accept my current station and just do the work. Funny enough, a month later, I approached our neighbor and offered her a job. Just like that, I had hired myself out of accounting.

I now see the seemingly trivial tasks completed by Esther after fasting as calculated, strategic, and daring acts made with the Helmet of Salvation protecting her from the fear that once kept her silent. The day she approached the king, she *dressed* in her royal attire. She *stood* in the inner courtyard. She *gained* the king's favor when he saw her. She *walked* to the king. She *touched* the gold scepter the king extended. She *spoke* when the king asked what she wanted, telling her she could have anything, even half of the kingdom. Scripture is specific. She took action. It is easy to pass by simple actions, but simple actions set the atmosphere for change.

Esther was also calculated in her response. She wasn't focused on how other people might approach the king with such an astounding request, let alone approach him at all. She didn't focus on the law, and she didn't focus on impending death. She didn't respond with a plea for her life or the lives of her people. She simply requested that he and Haman join her for a banquet she had prepared for them. The king accepted. Esther continued to work in her sphere by preparing the banquet while God worked in His.

Doing the work allowed me to gain confidence because I could see the fruits of my labor. With the Helmet of Salvation firmly on my head, my mind was focused on God's voice, and the battle in my mind was nearly silenced. I could clearly see that small accomplishments along the way had steamrolled, gaining traction over time, and had turned into bigger ones. Much like the two men who took their portioned talents and did more with them in Matthew 25:14–30, I realized that I had the responsibility to steward well what I had and invest in creating more—not bury myself under a mound of blankets. The veil of doubt lifted, and I saw myself as God saw me. I had been making difficult choices for the company for years. I saw that I had directed conversations, resolved issues, projected forward vision, and led our company toward goals. With one dramatic shift, God planted new seeds of thought in my mind that overshadowed the seeds of doubt. The battlefield shifted.

The Book of Esther continues with her not only saving her people from genocide but also creating laws, reversing the tide on the Jews' enemies, and instituting new customs of celebration. That is quite a long way from a young woman obedient to a hidden identity and crowned as queen for her beauty.

Walking with God

SHOT Show 2024: I sat upright, poised yet relaxed in an elegant chair. Across from me sat two well-regarded people from the industry, shrugging off their most recent meeting after a long day of many on the conference floor. My chief growth officer sat between us, and my newly hired chief operations officer was at my side. Over the next hour, my CGO and I volleyed topics of conversation in sync, highlighting the company's capabilities, projects, expertise, brand, story, successes, and growth points while our COO observed. I engaged, asked questions, connected points, and redirected until we exhausted the content and purpose of the meeting.

We walked the duo to the large double doors of our Las Vegas Palazzo Tower suite. Closing the door behind them, my team turned to one another and, with unmistakable glee, high-fived like we had just won a high-stakes poker game. I took out my phone and called John. We gave him the play-by-play, and as the excitement buzzed in the room, I silently thanked God, remembering how far I had come.

Seeking God brought me to a place of peace. Esther's turn to God reminded me that reliance on His strength is easier than reliance on myself. My dive into God's Word and prayer shielded my mind from the once pestilent thoughts and provided a new perspective to boldly walk in my identity as a student and child of God. He showed me there was lasting comfort in walking an initially unfamiliar path. He revealed the tools He had already given me and my responsibility to do something with them as a leader. Finally, He took me out of the shadows, He placed me on a stage, and I walked unabashedly with Him.

 **THE TRUTH**

"You were made for this."

"HIS DELIGHT IS IN THE LORD'S INSTRUCTION, AND HE MEDITATES ON IT DAY AND NIGHT. HE IS LIKE A TREE PLANTED BESIDE FLOWING STREAMS THAT BEARS ITS FRUIT IN ITS SEASON, AND ITS LEAF DOES NOT WITHER. WHATEVER HE DOES PROSPERS"

Psalm 1:2-3 (CSB).

"WHO KNOWS, PERHAPS YOU HAVE COME TO YOUR ROYAL POSITION FOR SUCH A TIME AS THIS"

Esther 4:14 (CSB).

ELISAH MCGEE

About the Contributor

ELISAH MCGEE is a dynamic leader carving a renewed path. She seeks God in all things, lives life to its fullest, and balances a hard work ethic with simple joys as a hopeful example to her four children.

A visionary, she founded Freedom Defense Group (FDG) in 2019, alongside her husband, to raise the standard of innovation with mission-ready solutions for the Department of Defense and state, local, and federal agencies. Its mission is to serve the brave men and women of the United States who sacrifice their lives to protect others and secure freedom. FDG does its part to ensure our warfighters make it safely home to their families.

As CEO, Elisah strategically aligns her company to exceed objectives by building infrastructure, guiding philosophy, positioning growth, and empowering leaders. Securing certification as a woman-owned small business, Elisah persistently strives to lead with honor and integrity while encouraging her team and peers to do the same.

She faithfully pursues challenges to catapult personal growth and shift paradigm thinking. Moving their beach family to a barren ninety-five-acre farm in rural Brookneal, Virginia, in 2020, Elisah and her husband rapidly renovated, built structures, and adopted a growing variety of livestock. Two short years later, they founded a 501(c)3 nonprofit organization called Mission Freedom Farm that set the framework for a healing place for leaders to rest and reinvigorate their missions. She and her husband recently purchased a third farm to host weddings and events as well as land to expand her nonprofit.

Elisah is an avid philanthropist and community advocate. She has served as an election official with the Virginia Department of Elections since 2020, was Mrs Virginia USA Earth 2023, and worked as a board member of Keep Virginia Beautiful.

A University of Virginia graduate, she is also a creative big-picture thinker and writer. She transcribed one hundred World War II letters between two sweethearts for her community, serves as a caretaker for two century-old cemeteries, and has been entrusted with transcribing and preserving another World War II military journal. Her time serving as Mrs Virginia USA Earth set her on a journey to write and publish her first children's book, *Be Kind to Nature*, in 2023.

7

Business Is War

By Chris Rickstrew

The Lie
"You're an Entrepreneur"

I was shocked, amazed, and excited, but most of all, I was ready to fight! After reading Matthew 10:34 (ESV), it was impossible for me not to feel these things. Jesus said, "Do not think that I have come to bring peace to the earth. I have not come to bring peace, but a sword." What?! Being new to the faith, I had always heard that Jesus was kind, loving, and, most of all, peaceful. So why was the "Prince of Peace" saying these words? Why was Jesus bringing a sword to the earth instead of peace?

My amazement and excitement went even deeper when I looked up the word *sword* in the original Greek. The Greek word for *sword* in Matthew 10:34 is *machaira*, which translates to "war!" Jesus himself said, "I have not come to bring peace, but [war]." In that moment, my life and perspective changed dramatically. I saw life differently. I read the Bible differently. But most of all, I did business differently.

If the King of kings and Lord of lords said that He came to bring war, then it's war that we're in. As an entrepreneur, we are called to go out into the world and solve some of the biggest problems that people struggle with. Every day of our lives is a battle to help other people. Every day of our lives, we are fighting to solve a problem for someone in need. And every day, we have to get up and push ourselves to grow, to step out of our comfort zones, and to make a difference in this world.

As entrepreneurs, we are used to the internal battle, but are we aware of the spiritual battle that we are engaged in? As an entrepreneur, you're not just a business owner, you're a warrior! Every day that you wake up and walk out that door, you step onto a battlefield. The world calls it business, but the Kingdom calls it a battle.

You don't have to read much of the Bible to see that God's people have spent most of their existence in some form of battle, whether physical or spiritual. As modern-day Christians, we are right in the middle of the most epic spiritual battle in the history of humanity! Never has there been more deception and evil in the world than today. But Jesus said, "Look, I have given you authority over all the power of the enemy, and you can walk among snakes and scorpions and crush them" (Luke 10:19, NLT). I truly believe that. I also believe that, as entrepreneurs, we have the opportunity to be some of the most influential people in the world. Through our products, people, and profits, we can expand the Kingdom of God and help fulfill the Great Commission in ways that the world has never seen. But to do that, we have to stop looking at ourselves, our customers, and our companies through the lens of the world and instead, start looking at them through the lens of the Kingdom.

The world does business one way, but the Kingdom does business another. As the Body of Christ, we are called to do business differently because we are called to see business differently. As the Body of Christ, we aren't obsessed with profits; we are obsessed with people. As the

"This isn't business, this is war!."

Body of Christ, we are here to fulfill the Great Commission, to go and make disciples of all nations (Matthew 28:16–20). When I had this realization, everything changed for me. I truly believe that when you have the same realization, everything will change for you as well. Jesus said you will "know the truth, and the truth will set you free" (John 8:32,

ESV). Well, the truth is that this isn't business; this is war! And you, my friends, are right in the middle of it; so welcome to the battle!

As you continue reading, I pray the Holy Spirit opens your eyes to see things from a fresh perspective—a fresh perspective for your company, your role, your products, your customers, and your impact. I pray the enemy's strongholds are torn down and chains are broken. I pray you feel convicted as well as encouraged. And I pray you walk away from this touched, transformed, and ready to fight like never before! Okay, let's dive in!

The Problem: You're Not Overcoming a Problem; You're Overcoming the Enemy!

As entrepreneurs, it's in our nature to look for solutions to the everyday problems we see in the world. Everywhere we go, we see problems, solutions, and potential businesses. When we see a problem, we search for a solution. And when we don't find an available solution, we create one. After we create that solution, we then create a business. However, as Christian entrepreneurs, we know that we're not actually dealing with problems; we're dealing with the enemy. We know the enemy is the source of most problems because the Bible says, "The thief comes only to steal and kill and destroy" (John 10:10, ESV). The problems that your customers face are either stealing something from them, killing something inside of them, or destroying something around them. So when we look at people struggling with problems in the world, what we see are people who are struggling with the enemy.

As entrepreneurs, we are not just finding solutions to the problems; we are actually creating weapons that defeat the enemy. This is a completely different way of thinking for most entrepreneurs. They see a problem and create a solution, which is their product. But as warriors, when we see a problem, we create weapons to overcome the enemy so people can stand in victory. In every battle, there's a hero and a villain. And in business, it's no different.

So how do you identify the enemy you are fighting against? It's simple; just ask yourself what is the number-one negative emotion your customers feel because of the problem they are facing. It could be fear, anxiety, overwhelm, sadness, scarcity, anger, frustration, smallness, insignificance, insecurity, doubt, etc. This question will give insight into the actual enemy you're fighting. The Word says, "For we are not fighting against flesh-and-blood enemies, but against evil rulers and authorities of the unseen world, against mighty powers in this dark world, and against evil spirits in the heavenly places" (Ephesians 6:12, NLT). Remember, your business doesn't just solve a problem; it fights against a spirit! And when you realize that you're fighting a spirit, you will realize that this is war and the products and services you offer are weapons equipping God's people to overcome the enemy and stand in victory.

I own a company called Warriors of God, and we help believers find their calling in life. When I was doing research for my business, I discovered that 89 percent of believers do not know their calling! I was absolutely shocked because there are so many sermons preached on this subject, yet the Body of Christ lacks clarity on a mass scale. I used to walk into church as an unbeliever and think to myself, "If you guys really have God on your side, then how are you not running the world?!" Well, the moment I read that statistic, I got the answer to my question. When a believer is not clear about who they are called to be and what they are called to do, they are immediately limited. Imagine if Noah wasn't clear about what God called him to build, and instead of building an ark, he built a house! None of us would be here.

What I discovered is the people I am meant to serve are being attacked by the spirit of confusion! As long as they are confused about what their calling is, they will never be able to live into it, and they are no longer a threat to the enemy. To combat the spirit of confusion, God gave me a Bible-based framework that helps any believer find their calling in just seven weeks! We combat the spirit of confusion with a framework that brings clarity. We identify the problem and provide a weapon!

The Customers: You Don't Have Customers; You Have Prisoners of War!

As entrepreneurs, we are really good at seeing problems and identifying the people struggling with those problems. These people end up being our customers, and we need to keep in mind that they are not just dealing with problems; they're dealing with the enemy. This realization allows us to look at our customers in an entirely new way. We can see them as "prisoners of war." These customers are struggling with a problem, and that problem is suppressing them and making their lives harder. They are held captive and become prisoners to the problem, just like in actual warfare. When an enemy force captures their opponents, they imprison them. They torture and destroy them. It's no different in the spiritual realm. Your customers (who are struggling with this problem you can solve) are prisoners in a spiritual war, and it is your job as the entrepreneur to give them the weapons they need to escape the prison. It is your job as the entrepreneur to help these prisoners of war overcome the enemy and stand in victory, and you do that with your products.

In my business, my customers are prisoners to the fact that they don't know their calling in life. When a believer doesn't know their calling, they tend to feel lost, stuck, unfulfilled, and frustrated. They know they have greatness inside of them, but they don't know how to step into it. And as long as the enemy holds them captive, they live the rest of their lives wasting their potential.

One of the most interesting things about your customers is that, in most cases, they were you before you solved the problem! Because of this, you will naturally have a deep passion to serve them. You know what it feels like to be a prisoner of this problem. Years ago, I was so lost and confused that I downsized my company, gave away all of my stuff, and went on a three-year soul-searching journey through Thailand, Bali, and Nepal, just trying to find my calling in life. Now I can save someone three years and help them find their calling in seven weeks! Your customers are prisoners of war, and your product is the key that unlocks their cell door!

The Products: You Don't Have Products; You Have Weapons!

Most entrepreneurs will offer a product or service and think it's just that. But in the spirit realm, these are not just products and services, they are weapons! And these weapons are designed specifically to help your customers escape the prison the enemy has them in. The world creates products to make a profit, but Kingdom entrepreneurs create products to help set people free. This is a completely different way of doing business—designing products and services with freedom in mind rather than profit. This way of thinking will lead to you creating something that has never been created before.

When I tell potential customers that I have a Bible-based framework that can help them find their God-given calling in just seven weeks, they are shocked! I was just as shocked when God gave it to me! The framework, combined with the coaching program, covers everything you need to discover who God has called you to be and what God has called you to do in this world:

- Step #1: We get clear on **who** you are called to be, which is made up of your identity, gifts, and values.
- Step #2: We get clear on **what** you are called to do in the world, which is made up of the problem you solve, the people you serve, and the vehicle you create.
- Step #3: We take all of those amazing revelations and create a **"calling statement,"** which allows you to clearly articulate your God-given calling in a single sentence!

From that moment on, your life is forever changed, and you become a massive threat to the enemy! I truly believe there is nothing more dangerous to the enemy than a believer who knows their calling. Your product or service is meant to be a weapon that helps your customers break free from the oppression of the enemy. When I see a believer gain clarity on their calling, I see one of God's warriors step into their greatness and never look back. It's one of the most rewarding experiences of my life. To see people set free inspires me more than any amount of profit ever could. But the beautiful thing is that I get to see people set free *and* make a profit at the same time! Your product is a weapon that will set God's people free while also providing for you, your family, and the expansion of God's kingdom.

The Company: You're Not Building a Company; You're Building an Army!

In the world, entrepreneurs build companies that create products, and those products solve problems for customers. But in the Kingdom of God, we build armies that create weapons, and those weapons help the prisoners of war defeat the enemy and stand in victory. In the world, companies are mainly designed to do one thing: make money. But in God's Kingdom, the focus of the army is to push back the enemy and set the captives free. Jesus told us to "go and make disciples of all nations" (Matthew 28:19, NLT). This command from Jesus, our commander-in-chief, is a command to go into enemy territory and rescue people who are in the darkness. In the world, we're here to fight for profits. In the Kingdom, we're here to fight for souls. But to do that, we need to build an army.

Jesus himself said that He came not to bring peace but war. And then He commanded us to go out into the world (enemy territory) and make disciples of all nations. With that being said, wouldn't it make a lot more sense to build an army rather than a company?! Armies operate differently than companies. Armies join together under a single cause and are willing to fight for what they believe in. Companies come together to solve a problem to make money. The reality is that we will all stand before Jesus one day, hoping to hear those amazing words: "Well done, my good and faithful servant" (Matthew 25:21, NLT). As I think about those words, I wonder if Jesus would be more impressed if I built a company or if I built an army. This is something that entrepreneurs need to think about regularly. Life is short compared to eternity, and nothing you create on this earth can be taken with you. But the impact you make stays in your spirit forever.

The Profits: You're Not Fighting for Profits; You're Fighting for People!

Being an entrepreneur is an incredible blessing, but it's also an incredible responsibility. God has entrusted us to create and steward something that has the potential to massively impact people all around the world. We can do it to make money, or we can do it to make a difference. We can do it to succeed in the world, or we can do it to succeed in the Kingdom. The amazing thing is that true success in the Kingdom leads to true success in the world! Jesus said, "But seek first the kingdom of God and his righteousness, and all these things will be added to you" (Matthew 6:33, ESV). When you seek the Kingdom of God, He will provide everything you need to be fruitful in your life and your business. In Matthew 6:24, it says, "No one can serve two masters. Either you will hate the one and love the other, or you will be devoted to the one and despise the other." It then goes on to say, "You cannot serve both God and money." As entrepreneurs, we walk a fine line between pursuing people and pursuing profits. But it is our duty and responsibility to steward the gifts that God has given us and help set the captives free.

Our adversary, Satan, is the father of lies and the master of deception. He would love nothing more than for you to devote your life to building a company that makes money in the world but doesn't make a difference in His Kingdom. But the Word says to "resist the devil, and he will flee from you" (James 4:7, ESV). And one of the greatest ways that we can resist the enemy is by knowing the truth and living it! The truth is that you're not here to build a company, you're here to build an army. And the moment you understand this, your perspective of your entrepreneurial journey will change forever. When you realize that you're building something for the King of kings and the Lord of lords, it is the greatest honor that you could ever receive. Jesus chose *you* to fight for the oppressed and lost. And He gave you a company and a product to do it with, which is an unbelievable blessing. We know that "many are called, but few are chosen" (Matthew 22:14, ESV), and I believe that even fewer say yes. Saying yes to God can be one of the scariest things we do as entrepreneurs, but it's also one of the most freeing and fulfilling.

The Entrepreneur: You're Not an Entrepreneur; You're a General!

I'll never forget the Sunday that shifted my identity forever. There I was in church, listening to a sermon from our pastor, but in my head, I was having a conversation with God—thinking about my company and wondering what to do next, where to go, what to build, what to create . . . and as I sat there, God said to me, "You're not building a company; you're building an army." The moment I heard those words, my heart cracked open in a way that it never had before. Truly, for the first time, my company became more about people than money. My company became more about the impact rather than income. And God allowed me to see my company and my future through my heart rather than my head. That's when my entire perspective shifted.

That's when I realized I wasn't solving a problem; I was defeating the enemy. I wasn't pursuing customers; I was freeing prisoners of war. I wasn't selling a product; I was offering a weapon. I wasn't fighting for profits; I was fighting for people. I wasn't building a company; I was building an army. But what opened my eyes most of all was when I realized that I wasn't an entrepreneur; I was a general! And so are you! The Word says for you to "Put on the full armor of God, so that you can take your stand against the devil's schemes. For our struggle is not against flesh and blood, but against the rulers, against the authorities, against the powers of this dark world and against the spiritual forces of evil in the heavenly realms" (Ephesians 6:11–12). You know what kind of person puts on armor every day to stand against the devil and his schemes? A general! You're a general in the army of God, and that is a completely different level of responsibility and one that you must take seriously. It's also a massive opportunity to be someone you've never been before and to do something you've never done before.

To the world, you're just an entrepreneur with a company that helps customers solve a problem with your products. But to His Kingdom, you're a general leading an army that equips the prisoners of war with weapons that will help them overcome the enemy and stand in victory! You're a general, fighting in the most epic spiritual battle, supporting the Body of Christ in fulfilling the Great Commission!

The Responsibility: It's Not Your Responsibility; It's Your Duty!

This isn't business; this is war. Every day as generals, we must put on the Helmet of Salvation and protect our minds from the lies of the enemy. If we don't, we will be led astray by Satan and will inevitably pursue money, power, status, and control. We will eventually see customers as numbers rather than souls. We have been saved, and the truth has set us free; therefore, we must stand in freedom by operating in truth. And the truth is that God has chosen you and entrusted you with so much more than you could ever imagine.

Jesus is your commander-in-chief, and by His grace, you will raise up an army, overcome the enemy, and help fulfill the Great Commission. Jesus came to bring war, and He chose you to reinforce the victory that He sealed for us on the cross. You've been given a divine assignment and an incredible gift

> "Jesus came to bring war, and He chose you to reinforce the victory that He sealed for us on the cross."

that allows you to take an idea from God and turn it into reality. God has given you the ambition, the motivation, and the determination to create something from nothing that will change people's lives. God has given you the creativity to think in a way that the world has never seen before. When you are chosen, you have God's favor. When you are chosen, you have God's victorious right hand on you and your company.

But it takes a new level of faith to let go of the company and focus on building what you're truly here to build: an army. It's so easy to be distracted and tempted by the money, the success, the respect, and the status. This is why we must keep our eyes fixed on Jesus as we run the race marked before us. As long as we do this, we will build what He's called us to build and help who He's called us to help. And if we stand in truth and build from that foundation, then one day, we will hear those glorious words: "Well done, good and faithful servant! You have been faithful with a few things; I will put you in charge of many things. Come and share your master's happiness!" (Matthew 25:21).

What you build is up to you. But just remember, your eternity will far outlast your company.

 **THE TRUTH**

"You're a General!"

"DO NOT THINK THAT I HAVE COME TO BRING PEACE TO THE EARTH. I HAVE NOT COME TO BRING PEACE, BUT A SWORD"

(Matthew 10:34, ESV).

"FOR THOUGH WE LIVE IN THE WORLD, WE DO NOT WAGE WAR AS THE WORLD DOES"

(2 Corinthians 10:3).

"PUT ON THE FULL ARMOR OF GOD, SO THAT YOU CAN TAKE YOUR STAND AGAINST THE DEVIL'S SCHEMES. FOR OUR STRUGGLE IS NOT AGAINST FLESH AND BLOOD, BUT AGAINST THE RULERS, AGAINST THE AUTHORITIES, AGAINST THE POWERS OF THIS DARK WORLD AND AGAINST THE SPIRITUAL FORCES OF EVIL IN THE HEAVENLY REALMS"

(Ephesians 6:11–12).

CHRIS RICKSTREW

About the Contributor

When Chris was twenty-seven, he had arrived at where he "thought" he wanted to be in life . . . and he was miserable! He was unhappy, unfulfilled, and completely lost.

This realization led him to downsize his company, give away all his stuff, and buy a one-way ticket to Nepal! He spent the next three years living in Nepal, Thailand, and Bali while trying to find his calling in life. But it wasn't until Chris started to pursue Jesus that clarity came! The Lord not only gave him clarity on his calling, but He also gave him a brilliant framework to help other believers do the same!

Today, Chris is a speaker, master coach, and founder of Warriors of God, a company that helps believers find their calling in just seven weeks! Chris knows that when a believer finds their calling, they become a *warrior*! And he is on a mission from God to raise up an army of warriors who will go out and fulfill the Great Commission!

Chris has a "Saul to Paul" testimony and is now completely on fire for God and fully committed to expanding the Kingdom! He has tried everything else out there and can truly say from experience that Jesus is the *only* way!

8

The Fruitful Life Equals
True Success

By Tierney Shirrell

The Lie
"The Be-Do-Have Model for Life Success"

"Where have you been?" I asked with exasperation. While I was deep breathing through the process of having a massive needle inserted into my spine, my husband had been MIA! This was our first baby, and he knew I was already terrified of the epidural, having never been too fond of needles. But while I mentally went to my happy place to get my mind off the sharp object being carefully inserted (so as not to cause life-altering consequences, including paralysis), the person who was supposed to be holding my hand was nowhere to be found.

"Um . . . out in the hallway, eating breakfast," he replied sheepishly. "Your parents brought me food." Fortunately for him, everything had gone as expected, and I was now resting without the pain of labor for the time being. In hindsight, God was probably protecting me—giving me a no-show partner as opposed to one passed out on the floor of the delivery room! As much as I hated needles and blood, I could handle them by averting my eyes; however, my husband had a history of fainting in their vicinity. So, the crisis averted, we could have a good laugh at the situation and dissipate the tension.

It's pretty hilarious to think that I once answered the question, "What do you want to be when you grow up?" with "a pediatrician." Once I found out about the human anatomy class that I'd need to take to pursue that profession, I was out! Can you recall some of your responses to these types of inquiries as a child? I'm not exactly proud to admit that "happy," "rich," and "a great mom" were some of the other answers I gave. Not that these are horrible, of course. I absolutely want to be a great mom, but how is that defined? And how are "happy" and "rich" defined, for that matter? We're doing our children and ourselves a disservice by asking these questions. The focus on what you must be and what you must do to have what you want has created a widely used framework for life success that's known as the Be-Do-Have model. We need to ask a better question, not just as parents but as humans and, more specifically, as children of God.

When I was graduating from high school, I was told my older cousin (the one who had the huge house, fancy cars, and traveled the world) was an engineer, but his wife, who was a CPA, made more money than he did—and sadly, that's how I chose my college major of accounting. It was not based on how I was uniquely designed to serve the world, and it wasn't even based on anything I was passionate about. Rather, it was solely based on the career path that was going

> **"The focus had always been on achieving..."**

to make me the most money and give me the life I always wanted, or so I thought. The focus had always been on achieving—from earning straight As, being in the National Honor Society, and serving as captain of the cheerleading squad, to receiving college scholarships, securing the highest-paid internship, and, ultimately, landing a successful accounting job. We spend our lives, from childhood onward, trying to gain approval and love in all the wrong ways, checking the boxes of education, career, marriage, parenting, and whatever accomplishments will bring the wealth, power, and status the world tells us will provide the life we've always wanted. The world says the Be-Do-Have model of life success is how we achieve the American Dream. We need to become someone we're not and do whatever it takes to "have it all," as society has defined it. The world says, "Be more, do more, have more." The Word of God says, "What good will it be for someone to gain the whole world, yet forfeit their soul?" (Matthew 16:26).

We can learn so much from the woman at the well about looking to worldly things to fill the void that can only be filled by Jesus. The Bible doesn't even give us her name, only that she was a Samaritan woman who was coming to the well during the middle of the day. This is significant because women typically drew water in groups during the cooler temperatures of early morning or late evening. This particular woman, however, chose to come when she would be alone, away from the judging eyes of others, because she was living in the shame of sin. The woman had been married many times, and she was currently living with a man she wasn't married to. She lived her life basing her worth on men, looking to them to give her status and satisfy her soul.

Are there things outside of Jesus that you've entrusted to give your life purpose, to give you your worth, or to satisfy your desires? I once heard the quote, "God gives us our heart's desires, and then He gives us our heart's desires." No, that's not a misprint. It's meant to be repetitive, but the two identical phrases have two different meanings. The first half of this quote means that He intentionally places those specific desires, unique passions, and ambitions in our hearts. The second half means that God fulfills those desires. Psalm 37:4 tells us, "Take delight in the Lord, and He will give you the desires of your heart." So the desires that God gives us are the ones that He put there to begin with, but in our human nature, which is susceptible to the enemy's deception, we put desires in our hearts as well. We need to check our hearts and guard them from sinful desires. The woman at the well encountered Jesus, who revealed himself as the "living water," the well that would never run dry, and the one who would always satisfy her every need. Jesus is the never-ending source that produces the fruits of the Spirit in our lives. Even two thousand years ago, this woman served as an example of today's societal norms that encourage you to be true to yourself, satisfy your desires in whatever way makes you happy, and consider wealth, power, and status as the ultimate goals in life. But if you are true to yourself, and your "self" is not anchored in Christ, your "self" will destroy you.

Jesus called out the Samaritan woman's sins with gentleness and offered her, without condemnation, the solution for her striving. Having experienced being truly seen, known, and loved, she ran off to tell everyone about this "living water." Scripture tells us that many of the Samaritans from that town became believers because of the woman's testimony. Jesus is unfazed by our sinful desires, just as He was by those of the woman at the well. And like her, He shows us the way to align our hearts' desires with the will of the Father and commissions us to go and spread the Good News!

The truth is that you don't need to be someone you're not or some new version of yourself that the world told you to be. Be who God made you to be! From the very beginning, even before you were formed in the womb, He knew exactly who He was creating— His masterpiece. He created us in His image to become more Christlike, and sometimes, that means un-becoming many of the things the world said we should be. It means shedding the labels we took on to become who we thought we had to be- to fit in, to be accepted, to feel good enough, to succeed, or to be loved. Remove the labels that don't line up with the Word of God. Release the shame of your past and remove the expectations to live up to a worldly definition of who you should be. Be who God made *you* to be!

> "He created us in His image to become more Christlike, and sometimes, that means un-becoming many of the things the world said we should be."

The truth is that you don't need to do whatever it takes or what you feel you must do; rather, do what God calls you to do! He calls each of us to the Great Commission, to love and serve others, and to become more like Jesus. God gives us unique callings and assignments to carry out that use our specific spiritual gifts, talents, abilities, life experiences, personality, passions, and desires.

But I have to lovingly burst your bubble for a moment—if you don't mind. Your talents were never meant for you. They were given to you by the God of the universe so that you could serve others and build His Kingdom. When you surrender control to God, when your growth is centered on faith in Jesus, when you rely on the power of the Holy Spirit, *watch out*! Failure, though it may appear that way to the world, is never the end of the story when God is the author. And God is the author of your story. You can do *nothing* apart from God, but you can do *all things* through Him who gives you strength (Philippians 4:13). God wants us to succeed in life.

The truth is that it's not about having the life you want. It's about having a fruitful life. When we operate in obedience to His will, God can do abundantly more than we could ask or even imagine—infinitely beyond our biggest prayers, deepest desires, wildest dreams, or highest hopes—according to the power that works in us (Ephesians 3:20). The power is already in us! What's that power? It's His Holy Spirit that produces the fruit in our lives, good fruit that includes love, joy, peace, patience, kindness, goodness, faithfulness, gentleness, and self-control (Galatians 5:22–23).

The Bible teaches us in Luke 6 that a bad tree will not bear good fruit, and a good tree will not bear bad fruit. Similarly, the good fruit of our lives comes from being rooted in Christ and is how the world will recognize us as Christ followers—not simply as believers or even children of God but as true followers who seek the will of God above all else and walk obediently in it. This is true success. And biblical success can certainly include things like wealth, power, and status—they just aren't the ultimate destination. To honor God, these things are only a means to an end of living a godly life and sharing that life with others.

Seek *first* His Kingdom and His righteousness, and *all these things* will be added to your life (Matthew 6:33). God meticulously designed you with gifts, talents, strengths, and abilities, and His blessings are on the other side of your obedience in using them to serve the world, not worldly success serving you.

So it's time to ask a better question than "What do you want to be when you grow up?" or "What do you want to do or have?" Instead, let's set up the future generation for success by asking better questions:

- How do you want to serve God and others?
- Where do your passions and your heart's desires match up with your gifts and talents?
- How do you want to use what God put inside you to create more followers of Jesus?

Have you ever asked yourself these questions? Or better yet, have you ever asked God how He wants you to serve, use your gifts, and make disciples? I've learned that continuous personal growth and development are essential to building a successful business and life, but it's time to disrupt that industry with a new Kingdom perspective. There comes a point when you realize that personal growth and development, or self-help (or whatever you want to call the process), means nothing if it's centered on you. Self-help is focused on just that—self. Seeking worldly success will leave you empty and striving. You may be growing, taking action, and accomplishing exciting things but, ultimately, if it depends on self—your strength, your abilities, your power—it's going to fail. These can only take you so far. We need to be willing to say, "This isn't about me; this is about me using what God has given me to bring Him glory." Success itself isn't the issue; rather, it's what the world has defined as success.

The Sword of the Spirit, which is the Word of God (Ephesians 6:17), is the first offensive weapon of the armor of God that we're told to put on as Christians—armor that is to be used to defeat the enemy, his temptations of worldly desires, and his attacks on our divine callings. By growing our faith, trusting in the Lord, and defining our success through the Word, and not the world, we can be strengthened to fulfill His will for our lives. So flip the traditional Be-Do-Have model on its head and redefine the formula for life success as . . .

 **THE TRUTH**

"Be who God made you to be. Do what God called you to do. Have a fruitful life!"

"BUT I SAY, WALK BY THE SPIRIT, AND YOU WILL NOT GRATIFY THE DESIRES OF THE FLESH. FOR THE DESIRES OF THE FLESH ARE AGAINST THE SPIRIT, AND THE DESIRES OF THE SPIRIT ARE AGAINST THE FLESH, FOR THESE ARE OPPOSED TO EACH OTHER, TO KEEP YOU FROM DOING THE THINGS YOU WANT TO DO"

(Galatians 5:16–17).

"BUT THE FRUIT OF THE SPIRIT IS LOVE, JOY, PEACE, PATIENCE, KINDNESS, GOODNESS, FAITHFULNESS, GENTLENESS, SELF-CONTROL; AGAINST SUCH THINGS THERE IS NO LAW. AND THOSE WHO BELONG TO CHRIST JESUS HAVE CRUCIFIED THE FLESH WITH ITS PASSIONS AND DESIRES"

(Galatians 5:22–24, ESV).

TIERNEY SHIRRELL

About the Contributor

TIERNEY SHIRRELL is the founder of the Live BOLD Movement community and ministry that empowers women to intentionally live **BOLD**-ly: **b**rave, **o**bedient, **l**oving, and **d**isciplined. She is a podcaster, host of events and retreats, and a number-one Barnes & Noble international best-selling author of *The Joy-Full Entrepreneur: Solutions, Signs, and Wonders*. She hosts the *Live BOLD Movement* podcast and has been a guest on *Real Faith Stories*, *Finding Your Fit*, and *Next Level Faith* podcasts as well as FaithTalk Radio. Tierney has been a featured speaker at the Live BOLD Retreat, the AWAKE Conference, and FounderCon.

She developed the Live BOLD Framework through her unique experiences, spanning from the corporate world to motherhood to entrepreneurship, all overshadowed by a mental health journey. Tierney activates women to boldly step into their unique God-given callings through prayer-powered personal growth mentorship. She has her master's degree and is a Certified Mentally Strong Coach. Tierney has done missionary work in Jamaica and loves to travel. She enjoys exploring Arizona, where she resides with her husband of eighteen years and their three kids.

9

The Power of the "And": You Are as Multidimensional as Your Creator

By Brittany Stinson

The Lie
"You Must Choose One"

You Are Not One-Dimensional

Have you ever felt like you are "just a mom" or "just an athlete?" Maybe you feel like your job only wants you for that one skill, or you're only known for that one thing, or you only get hired to solve that one problem. And maybe you're starting to believe there is only one thing you're good at and everything else is secondary. So to be successful, you'll just stick to "the one." Well, I'd like to invite you to a new idea today: you are like your Creator—multidimensional.

God exists in more than one dimension at all times. He is within us, around us, ahead of us, and He was before us. And, like Him, you are just as multidimensional. Limiting yourself to one dimension is to cut off some of the most impactful, beautiful, and life-changing parts of you.

- **God is within us:** In the same way that He is living on the inside of you (by the way, you're as close as you'll ever be to God, so take comfort in knowing He's always near), you have heart, passion, and skills inside you that will take you exactly where you want to go.

- **God is around us:** In the same way that He surrounds you and protects you, you Know (I like to say big *K*, like an inner God-sense of deep knowing) who and what are best to surround yourself, your family, and your business with to see them flourish and stay healthy.

- **God is ahead of us**: In the same way that He already knows the best steps for you to take, you have the same ability to tune into your God-given intuition and leadership capabilities to walk the road of life and business with powerful steps.

- **God was before us:** In the same way that He was here long before you were, you can look back at your past and see the tapestry woven into your life's story. A tapestry that holds wisdom, knowledge, experience, and lessons to share with others.

These are all different dimensions of God that are also a part of who you are, and limiting yourself to just one dimension will cut off so much of what you have to offer the world. Seeing yourself in a multidimensional light is the foundation of a fulfilled life and business. Let me use a fun illustration to further elaborate.

My family and I love the movie Inside Out. There is a scene in the movie where Joy and Sadness are on a journey through Abstract Thought, a place where Riley's thoughts and memories are deconstructed into abstract representations. This scene takes place when Joy and Sadness are trying to return to headquarters after getting lost in Riley's mind.

As they pass through Abstract Thought, they encounter a zone where everything becomes two-dimensional. Objects and characters flatten out, losing their depth and texture. Joy and Sadness, too, are affected by this transformation, becoming flattened versions of themselves. The scene plays out with some drama, some laughs, and is really a visually striking moment as Joy and Sadness struggle to navigate through this two-dimensional space. Their usual lively and expressive selves are reduced to simple outlines, emphasizing the absurdity of the situation. It serves as both a fun and funny moment in the movie as well as a creative exploration of the complexities of human thought and emotion.

Just like Joy and Sadness, we lose our "depth and texture" when we limit ourselves to just one dimension.

Let me illustrate a little further using the many names of Jesus. We know Jesus by so many names, i.e., dimensions of His character and personality. He was a carpenter *and* the great I Am. He was Jesus *and* the Lamb of God. He was the Judge *and* the Advocate, the King of kings *and* the Son. Some additional names of Jesus include:[4]

Savior	Redeemer	Bread of Life
Lord	Creator	Son of the Living God
Only Begotten Son	Holy One of Israel	Wonderful Counselor
Mighty God	Everlasting Father	Prince of Peace
Head of the Church	The Almighty	Alpha and Omega
Master	King of the Jews	High Priest
Prophet	Teacher	Immanuel
Mediator	Chief Cornerstone	Author and Finisher of Our Faith
The Good Shepherd	The Shepherd and Bishop of Souls	The Word
Fountain of Living Waters	The Rock	Messiah
The True Vine	The Branch	The Bridegroom
Dayspring	Shiloh	The Lion of the Tribe of Judah
The Bright and Morning Star	The Image of the Invisible God	Son of Man
The Way, the Truth, and the Life	King of Israel	Christ

---

4 "50 Names and Titles of Jesus Christ." The Church of Jesus Christ of Latter-Day Saints, accessed Aug. 8, 2024, https://www.churchofjesuschrist.org/comeuntochrist/believe/jesus/50-names-for-jesus.

I hope you can see by now that you are just like your Creator and that the One who made you made you in His image. He made you with depth, with multiple passions, and with an array of likes and things that excite you. He called you to reach and impact great numbers of people— people who will resonate with different aspects of who you are in your most authentic self.

And, by the end of this chapter, I hope you'll see that the most profitable, impactful, and fulfilling way to do life and business is to allow those you're called to reach to see *all* of who you are.

Let's bust the myth that you have to pick just one lane to win in business.

Multidimensional Business Growth

The day I deleted my business IG (Instagram) account was a big day for me. Although that account was new and I was in the launch phase of a new venture, it was a big faith step. I was essentially saying, "I will be just as successful in my business if you see all of me as I would be if you only saw the business side of me."

When I initially created it, it took a lot for me to put myself out there and say, "Hey world, I'm in business!" I had been in administrative and support roles for so long that putting

BRITTANYASTINSON
Posts
Follow

brittanyastinson ...

♡ 3 ○ ▽ 🔖

brittanyastinson Peace out, business page. Follow me @brittany_stinson to see my business, family, and real life - fully integrating things over here! I can't... more
March 28, 2022

my name on a website and standing up to bet on myself felt like a big step. So it felt safe to separate the business side of me from the rest of me. It was like a fresh start. But, ultimately, I found it lacked so much depth and texture (just like Joy and Sadness found that day) that there was very little traction. Based on what I was posting, the audience I was trying to build had little to resonate with and little common ground to stand on with me.

I've found that entrepreneurship is one of the greatest magnifying glasses for the internal "stuff" we all have to work through. So deciding to stop using my "biz-only" IG account was a representation of the internal work I was going through in my journey of confidence and self-worth. But I still had questions. Will people still respect me as a business owner when I post photos of my kids? Can I post pictures when I'm not in full hair and makeup and still grow this account? What if my family members are the only ones who comment on my business marketing posts? I was growing through all of those doubts and questions while leaning into God, trusting that when I showed people all of me, I would be more than enough to still be a leader and authority in my field.

> **"I've found that entrepreneurship is one of the greatest magnifying glasses for the internal "stuff" we all have to work through."**

Thankfully, today, I can say that I've grown and healed enough to share all sides of me with my audience. And, as you could've guessed, people become clients because they resonate with those many sides. Over the last three years (since I deleted that other Instagram account), my revenue has tripled. When I'm on discovery calls, I get to chat about my kids. When I'm onboarding clients, we get to connect on my posts about my workouts and my smoothies. And the best part is I realized that I am at the center of my business, and all of these sides of me are what make my business work so well. So it's *helpful* to express and coach through all areas of my life because that's how I'm successful, anyway! Why leave out the rest of your life when that's what is driving your revenue and connections?

Now, meet Kasey. Kasey will be our case study today as we explore this principle of "biz" me vs. "me" me more deeply.

Kasey is thirty-five years old, married, and has one young son. She is a new entrepreneur who just ventured out into her industry. Kasey has been following you on social media for a while, interacting with your content. Sometimes, she even sends messages of appreciation for things that resonate with her from your page and posts because they are helping her as she launches her new business. Through fear and doubt, she's going for it, and you're helping her through your content, even though she's not your client.

In marketing, there's lots of talk about the journey of "know, like, and trust." As someone enters your corner of the internet world, you begin to "nurture" them, and they start down a path with you—getting to know you, really starting to like you, and, if all goes well, trusting you. Trust is where the magic happens.

Now I want to play out two scenarios for a brief moment.

> Scenario #1: You've decided you're going for it online with your business. You're going to be an expert, a leading authority in your space, and you've decided to only post and write business content. This is what you're selling, and you want people to know the value you bring to the market. Family, friends, food, and gym pics have no place here! You're in business, after all. Kasey is inspired by your business help. She's getting so much value. She's promoting her business, she's making good hires, and her profits are going up. She's winning at her new biz venture.

> Scenario #2: All of the above is still true. You're really going for it online with your business. You are a leading authority, and people seek out your page for advice in your niche ("neesh"). But you have also committed to showing up and being transparent and authentic, allowing yourself to be seen

in all areas of your life. Your audience gets to see you on your health journey with sweaty gym pics. They get to see your kids' first day of school, and they get to support you on the hard days when you allow them behind the curtain just a little bit. Kasey is seeing all of the same results in her business (marketing is great, profits are going up, client base is growing). *And* she's having important conversations with her husband and family about how she feels. She's slowing down to connect with her son. She started seeing a counselor, and she's opening up and finding healing in her heart and spirit. Her life *and* business are improving because she's inspired by your authenticity and everything you allow her to see.

In Scenario #1, Kasey saw maybe a quarter of who you are and how you can be of value to her life. Therefore, you only helped Kasey at a quarter of the capacity that you could have. In Scenario #2, Kasey saw the majority of who you are, and therefore, you served Kasey at an increased capacity, in more areas of life where God has gifted you.

When we're allowed to interact with all sides of you—the human side as well as the business side—we will surely *know* you more, *like* you more, and *trust* you more deeply. The facade that we create to separate ourselves in business from the real us is exhausting and confusing. Didn't God make me in all the ways that I am—my business acumen *and* my personal side?

Simply put, I know God doesn't make mistakes. So, if it's true, that He created me to be multidimensional (the same way He is), and He gave me these different desires in my heart, and He's led me through various experiences in my life that have shaped me into who I am . . . then I can safely trust Him to let it *all* be expressed. In fact, the more I express each dimension of myself, the more people He can help through me. Yup, that sounds great! And it's a whole lot easier than having two IG accounts and perfectly positioning myself with each tidy piece of content every day.

Things Aren't That Fragile

A few years ago, I went through a purpose discovery course in my church. It was a church-wide initiative that every small group (life group) in our church was going through. My husband Darryll even got to help develop the curriculum with our senior pastor. Darryll and I were leading a life group of married couples at the time. We were so excited about this purpose campaign. We just knew that so many people were going to find their true God-given purpose and live and walk in freedom after going through this training. There were talks of some quitting their jobs, some leaving careers, some going back to school, and some wanting to go into ministry. Oh, my! Week over week, so much excitement was building. We heard about purpose during the sermons on Sunday and then attended our life groups throughout the week and went deeper into the material.

One Friday night, sitting on the floor at the home of the sweet couple hosting our life group, my workbook was open as I led a woman through the following questions:

- "What would you do if you knew you couldn't fail?"
- "What would you do if money were no object?"
- "What would you do if you knew you had your family's unconditional support and love?"

Her answers were amazing. They were vulnerable. They were real. But they weren't leading us to *one* thing. I asked follow-up questions and dug deeper into certain areas, hoping a common denominator would show itself obvious. I felt that if I couldn't pinpoint her *one* purpose, then the mission had failed. Somehow along the way, we had taken the material that was meant for deeper self-discovery of the gifts and talents given by God to enhance our purpose and made it a test that should spit out one right answer at the end.

At the end of our conversation, that woman looked at me a bit disheartened, a bit confused, and certainly deflated. "I guess I don't know what I'm supposed to do," she said—as if there was a singular path the material should've revealed to her about her next steps in fulfilling God's calling on her life. And because it was still unclear, I knew she felt she was going to *miss* what God had called her to.

The thought that you could miss out on your God-given purpose because you're unsure of your next step or because you can't firmly plant your flag in the ground and declare, "This is my purpose!"—oh my goodness, my heart still aches thinking about it.

Final Thoughts

No, no, no, my friend. Our multidimensional Creator, our heavenly Father, who loves you more deeply than you love your children, more deeply than your mother loves you— His plan for your life is not that fragile, and He is not that rigid. You will not, I repeat, *not* miss out on the plans God has for your life if you are unsure of your next step. <<Note to Designer: pull out the sentence before this for callout box: "You will not, I repeat, *not* miss out on the plans God has for your life if you are unsure of your next step. ">>Life is not a multiple-choice test with only one right answer.

> "You will not, I repeat, not miss out on the plans God has for your life if you are unsure of your next step."

I believe God is far more interested in who you are becoming from the inside out than He ever will be with the external business and life choices you make. If you are healing, if you are growing, if you are displaying His love and grace more often than not—this pleases the Father. And it's from that place of healing, of growing, of love, and of grace that you can operate your business, lead your family and your teams, make investments, speak to audiences, and make the impact you are called and created to make. You can do it under the title of "founder and CEO" or the title of "ice cream shop owner." There's no right answer as long as *you* are expressing your authentic self and displaying God's grace, love, and power through it all.

I am a wife, a mother, a daughter, a sister, a speaker, a business owner, a student, a guide, and a leader. The Belt of Truth is a representation of the full truth, and Scripture says that "the truth will set you free" (John 8:32). So while we may be good at one thing or called to one area, that's a partial truth. The full truth is that we are multidimensional, just like our Creator, whose image we are made in.

So, as you step into action, vulnerably express all of who you are, show the world the different sides of you, and courageously combine the "biz" you with the "you" you. And know that God will make your "and" go further than your "one thing" ever could have.

THE TRUTH

"The world needs all of you."

"FOR YOU CREATED MY INMOST BEING; YOU KNIT ME TOGETHER IN MY MOTHER'S WOMB. I PRAISE YOU BECAUSE I AM FEARFULLY AND WONDERFULLY MADE; YOUR WORKS ARE WONDERFUL, I KNOW THAT FULL WELL"

(Psalm 139:13–14).

"SO NOW THROUGH THE CHURCH THE MULTIFACETED WISDOM OF GOD [IN ALL ITS COUNTLESS ASPECTS] MIGHT NOW BE MADE KNOWN [REVEALING THE MYSTERY] TO THE [ANGELIC] RULERS AND AUTHORITIES IN THE HEAVENLY PLACES"

(Ephesians 3:10, AMP).

BRITTANY STINSON

About the Contributor

BRITTANY STINSON, MSA, is a speaker, operational strategist, and cofounder of Seeding Greatness. Struggling to find herself in college, Brittany overcame alcoholism and unhealthy relationships and went on to build a movement of leaders who impact the world with their stories. Brittany has worked with a diverse portfolio of clients, ranging from solopreneurs and student leaders to hospitals with $500-million-salary budgets. When she isn't working, Brittany enjoys working out and spending quality time with her husband and four children (preferably on a beach somewhere).

10

Deadly Perseverance

By Brittney Tollinchi

The Lie
"Quitting Is Failure"

The feeling pulsated through my brain. "This isn't the life I was meant to be living."

The anxiousness boiled in my heart. "I'm in the wrong place."

The longing in my soul screamed, "There has to be more to life than this!"

The realization poured over me in waves of guilt, shame, and utter confusion. I had done everything "right," everything "they" said to do:

Study hard—check.
Get a stable job—check.
Be a loyal spouse—check.
Go to church—check.
Be an attentive parent—check.
Keep climbing the ladder—check.

And yet, the exhausting numbness of waking up before the sun, putting in some work hours, trying to eat well, putting in more work hours, being present at home, running to after-school activities, slamming some dinner, making time for my spouse, and going to bed—just so that I could repeat it all the next day—ate at the depths of my soul.

On the outside, my life appeared to meet all of the "good-life" qualities, but inside, an awakening in my heart was growing. "For those who live according to the flesh set their minds on the things of the flesh, but those *who live* according to the Spirit, the things of the Spirit" (Romans 8:5, NKJV).

I'll never forget that road trip. It was supposed to be an easy eight-hour drive from Denver to Kansas City for the conference I would be attending for the weekend. As I headed out of town, the city fell into the distance, and the busyness of the world seemed to fade—no music, no work calls, no to-do list, no "Mommy can you . . ." Just me. As the silence deepened with every mile, the realization hit me.

I bawled for the duration of the 605-mile trip, tears streaming down uncontrollably in an emotional, physical, and mental release I didn't realize I needed. I was trying to work hard. I was trying to "mom" hard. I was trying to "wife" hard. I was trying to be everything for everyone (while also attempting to eat right and exercise—yay me). I was hustling in the American Dream and, undoubtedly, a lifetime of checking-off-the-boxes living had held me captive in the rut of simply surviving.

He was tugging on my heart, telling me that I was meant for more; I was created to thrive not just survive. But how did I get here, just moving through life on autopilot? Like many, I had been programmed to persevere—persevere when things get tough, persevere through the hurt, persevere through the doubt, persevere through the exhaustion, and persevere through the grief.

Even as bouncing baby boys and girls, we go from standing to taking our first steps, and our overjoyed parents start preaching to us, "Good job!" "Just one more, just one more step!" We are encouraged to keep going, to take just one more step, and to never quit. Before we know it, we're walking and running like pros.

But . . . when are we ever urged to quit walking or taught how to sit and be present in the stillness?

"IN REPENTANCE AND REST IS YOUR SALVATION; IN QUIETNESS AND TRUST IS YOUR STRENGTH"

(Isaiah 30:15).

There is, indeed, a time and place for everything.

Continuing on our adolescent journey, we start playing sports, joining clubs, learning to play instruments. We're urged to keep practicing so that we can get better, become talented in our crafts, and maybe even have a victory or two. One of my father's favorite stories to recall is when I persevered through bodily injury to practice my gymnastics skills until my hands bled, literally. Believe me; it took me months to even master a decent cartwheel as a freshman in high school, so an Olympic medal was never, ever in my future. Nonetheless, I was celebrated and praised for my hard work, determination to excel, and refusal to quit.

The sweetness of the victories and the continued praise became fuel to keep going. Quitting was a thing for losers, even amid exhausted efforts, disconnected passions, and the deepening value of meeting the expectations of what "they" said victory looked like. Are we ever taught that it's OK to quit? Maybe at the end of the season or after the final annual concert? Finish when the work is done, right?

In adulthood, when is the work *ever* done? When are there ever enough hours in the day to accomplish all of the to-dos and obtain those victories and sweet rewards promised on the other side of battling the uphill climb to glory—glory the enemy has spent my entire life convincing me I'd find in the form of the worldly desires of power in a title, status in a salary, or hope in a business revenue target?

I was never told to quit; instead, I was urged to keep hustling, keep grinding. While there is no doubt this perseverance programming had served me well in some areas of my life, there I was at the crossroads, questioning who I was, who I wanted to be, and if the hamster-wheel life was really the dream. Ephesians 2:8–9 reminds us, "For it is by grace you have been saved, through faith—and this is not from yourselves, it is the gift of God—not by works, so that no one can boast." What was I working so hard for, and what was it costing me?

Early in my career, about a decade before the Kansas City drive, I became aware of how much I tied my value, my self-worth, and who I was to a fancy job title, six-figure salary, and corner office. Whenever I was asked what I did for work (a very natural question when first introduced to anyone), I'd always respond, "I am a recruiting and sales manager."

I had been hustling through project season, which meant I was operating on overdrive, working fifteen-hour days at my desk, and oblivious to anything other than hitting the numbers. This meant breakfast, lunch, and dinner were also secondary to making "just one more call." In a supportive act of love, my spouse surprised me at the office with dinner. As I stepped away for just a brief moment to slam my fajita bowl, I felt a sense of pride. "Look at us putting in the hours and doing whatever it takes to succeed," I said. "This is what it takes to win! I'll do just one more hour and then be home." Just as soon as the pride had swelled in my chest, a gut-wrenching feeling dropped into my belly (and it wasn't just from eating too fast). I had become the girl who was willing to sacrifice my time, my body, and my relationships for work. For a job. For a paycheck. For dinner at a conference room table. I was living my life as though I was just "a recruiting and sales manager."

How deeply the enemy weaves lies into the pieces of our hearts where we hold our identity. While my autopilot "I am" response seemed innocent by nature (9.9 out of ten people will answer that what-do-you-do question with an "I am" statement), I recognized the bondage this statement imprisoned me in and the way my language held me back from living as the woman God created me to be. Beyond work, I was someone's significant other. I was someone's friend. I was someone's sister. But above all, I was God's daughter who was missing out on the beauty of allowing myself to *be* all of those things because I was pouring all of me into a J.O.B.

This was the first time I realized that self-sabotaging, to put in "just one more hour," was not rooted in goodness, righteousness, or truth. In fact (and I believe we all witness this regularly in our current culture), "just one more hour" had become costly to the pursuit of goodness, righteousness, and truth. It was one more hour spent at the office instead of playing with the kids. It was one more hour spent entertaining a business partner instead of connecting with a spouse waiting at home. It was one more hour spent persevering . . .

I began to make some changes in setting boundaries and better managing my time. One such change occurred in the language I used. I started talking about my work based on the verb associated with what I was doing and not the job title (e.g., "I *manage* recruiting and sales teams"). I quit a piece of my worldly identity and pressed forward in who He said I was.

Fast-forward to the Kansas City drive where I was again receiving another wake-up call. This time, although confident in my identity in Him, I found myself in a state of exhaustion, confusion, and even anger. As an innate high achiever, I had been grinding and hustling so hard. I was stuck on autopilot and in survival mode. How could this be what life was all about? The cost of this autopilot, hustle-and-grind life had detoured me from His greater purpose and living out His plan for my life. I could feel it moving in my soul, like the tears streaming down my face.

I had started to believe that life was just predestined for struggle instead of faithfully knowing that I was a living, breathing, walking being with direct access to the One Most High God and divinely created with a plan in mind. "'For I know the plans I have for you,' declares the Lord,

'Plans to prosper and not to harm you, plans to give you hope and a future'"(Jeremiah 29:11).

The enemy's lies about my identity and a life of struggle were thrust toward me, like fiery arrows. I had become distracted by empty promises of victories and sweet rewards on the other side of deadly perseverance in worldly endeavors. I knew I desperately wanted to pivot back into alignment with His plan and my God-given purpose.

But that would require ... quitting.

Reconnecting and realigning to my purpose would require quitting— quitting the piece of my journey that I was merely meant to pass through and never be stuck in, quitting the fixated longing and loyalty to my worldly endeavors and check-the-box accomplishments, quitting the denial of who God created me to be, what He created me for, and the plan He etched on my soul long before my first breath.

In Genesis 12:1, God calls Abraham to "Go from your country, your people and your father's household to the land I will show you." Although older in years and filled with great uncertainty, Abraham trusted God's plan and promise of blessings. He carried out the commands in obedient surrender, and God fulfilled His promise to make Abraham the father of many nations.

Quitting isn't failure. Quitting is freedom through obedient surrender.

Look at the other heroes of the Bible, and you'll see each had a story that required the utmost surrender in faith, as they were asked to quit their plans to answer their purposed callings (Moses, Peter, and Jeremiah, to name a few).

> **"Quitting isn't failure. Quitting is freedom through obedient surrender."**

"DO NOT CONFORM ANY LONGER TO THE PATTERN OF THIS WORLD, BUT BE TRANSFORMED BY THE RENEWING OF YOUR MIND. THEN YOU WILL BE ABLE TO TEST AND APPROVE WHAT GOD'S WILL IS—HIS GOOD, PLEASING AND PERFECT WILL"

(Romans 12:2).

This kind of surrender requires faith. It cannot be done without it. Within this act, His strength becomes our own, and His hope and enlightenment radiate through. We open our hearts to be known by Him and, in turn, know Him better. In our surrender, we become willing and able to open our hearts in love and accept His grace to live a life of peace.

When we pick up our Shield of Faith, we can confidently press forward in peace. Peace that He is with us. Peace that He is exactly who He says He is because He keeps His promises. Peace that He has a beautiful plan for our lives, and it's full of abundance. Peace that, in Him, we will find all of the strength, courage, and bravery we need to walk with Him in the plan for our lives. Peace that He goes before us, behind us, and beside us every step of the way. Peace that the enemy's arrows are merely tufts of cotton being tossed at an impenetrable plate of steel.

Step into faith and let Him grant you peace.

In a world full of available abundance, why are we willing to put ourselves through so much pain by denying our gut instincts, lying about what we know is true, and refusing what He put in our hearts?

"In a world full of available abundance, why are we willing to put ourselves through so much pain by denying our gut instincts, lying about what we know is true, and refusing what He put in our hearts?"

135

Why do we choose the comfort of the hell we know versus accepting the grace and goodness of His real plan for our lives? Why do we remain in survival mode instead of thriving? The simple answer is that we've become distant from His Truth. The enemy has infected our minds with distractions, fixed our hearts on empty endeavors, and tainted our souls with false identities. If we persevere on this path, the cost will be death—mentally, physically, emotionally, and spiritually. Deadly perseverance.

The only way off this fatal trajectory is to quit. Obediently surrender in faith, in exchange for your freedom. But how?

Repent. Be still. Recalibrate.

His call for my repentance was the moment I felt the anxiousness boiling in my heart. This wasn't the life I was meant to live. I was exhausted, and I knew I would have to give and receive forgiveness for this stubborn tiredness and for how distant I had become from Him. I had to take a closer look at my life and rethink the areas where I was in a constant state of exhaustion and stress: my job, certain relationships, and my physical health. And in His graciousness through this process, He revealed, in beautiful moments of awareness, the areas in my life where I was still at peace and energized: my marriage, certain relationships, and my personal growth.

But if this autopilot, survival-mode life wasn't intended for me, then what was, and who would I be instead?

I had to quit looking for these answers in all the wrong external places and become willing to accept that my answers would be found in Him, the One who lives in me. The best way for me to reconnect with Him was to reconnect with myself in stillness—to listen to the goodness of the desires etched on my heart, to lean forward into the righteousness of walking in faith first, and to reclaim the identity He gave me.

This was the toughest part of my journey. My default perseverance programming had convinced me that working and grinding to exhaustion were the keys to tapping into a life of abundance. Taking time to "be still" would require me to quit overbooking schedules, overextending efforts, over-communicating boundaries, and overexerting busyness.

It wasn't easy, and it required intentional effort to create space where I could literally quit the busyness of life (wake up, work, kids, spouse, eat, repeat). I started making small habit changes, like journaling or meditating, instead of logging into work early. Sometimes, it was a difference of just fifteen minutes, but fifteen minutes with God can solve a lifetime of problems. I started spending a lot more time in prayer and asking God to guide my decisions about big projects, organizational moves, and where my personal time needed to be spent (guilt-free).

The more stillness I created in my life through prayer, journaling, and meditation, the more space there was to hear Him, to feel Him, and to reconnect to my center and what I knew to be true about our loving God and His promises.

"'YOU WILL SEEK ME AND FIND ME WHEN YOU SEEK ME WITH ALL YOUR HEART. I WILL BE FOUND BY YOU,' DECLARES THE LORD"

(Jeremiah 29:13–14).

Repentance and stillness rejuvenated my faith.

The pulsating of "I'm in the wrong place" was turned into a feeling that I can only describe as comfort and gratitude. A lifetime of moments had been divinely crafted for me so that He could meet me in my survival and remind me that He keeps His promises. He hadn't forgotten about me in my tiredness or in the distraction of my worldly pursuits. As I again picked up my Shield of Faith, I gained His strength, His bravery, and His courage to passionately pursue what I knew to be true: there has to be more to life than this.

Recalibration requires movement. It's one thing to possess knowledge, but it's quite another thing to possess the ability to act, especially if it requires quitting. Quitting a career I had dreamed of and dedicated so much of my life to was one of the most difficult actions that I knew was required of me to step back into who God was calling me to be. Besides going completely against my prior programming, the initial thought of quitting a stable and prestigious dream job seemed stupid, lonely, and scary.

The enemy's arrows fire toward those willing to advance and walk in God's Word.

With shield in hand, I pressed forward against the criticism, the lack of understanding, the fear of the unknown, the fear of failure, and the fear of lack—walking in obedient surrender. And as He promised, I found *rest* in this surrender. Rest for my heart that was longing to be in alignment with His. Rest in knowing I wasn't on this journey alone and never had been. Rest in knowing I was divinely held, cared for, and intentionally designed for the life ahead of me. The more I surrendered, the greater *peace* I found.

A lot of us are persevering on the wrong path. We're lost. We're broken . . . but we keep refusing to quit. We have to decide: deadly perseverance or obedient surrender? I'd rather quit in the glory of His grace and love than live in the exhausted numbness of worldly expectations.

"And we know that in all things God works for the good of those who love him, who have been called according to his purpose" (Romans 8:28).

We all get stuck, multiple times over, in our lives. But will you quit the right things so that you can step into the beauty and abundance of His freedom? Will you quit checking the boxes and stop chasing what the world is telling you to do? Will you quit a life on autopilot? Will you quit forcing an identity that isn't aligned with who He says you are? Will you quit denying the life He created for you?

He is waiting for us to quit and abandon the pursuit of a personal plan that is out of alignment with His greater calling on our lives.

He is waiting for us to obediently surrender, to accept His gifts in the identity He gave us, and to step fully into who He created us to be in a life that He beautifully and intentionally orchestrated for us through His love, His grace, His kindness, and His faith in us that we'd seek Him.

Surrender in our faith. Be obedient in our awakening.

Pick up your Shield of Faith, and walk in confidence that what He has designed for you is the same righteous calling that is pulling at your heart. In Him, you'll have the bravery and courage to release the worldly identity you've been locked into. You'll hear the releasing click of the shackles that you have borne the weight of every day. And, even in your fears of the unknown, you'll know that you are divinely held in His goodness. "And who knows but that you have come to your royal position for such a time as this?" (Esther 4:14).

He created you to rise up and quit.
He created you to be strong and quit.

He created you to step into abundance and quit the life that "isn't the life you were meant to be living." Allow that feeling of "I'm in the wrong place" to be your clarion call to make a change. He's waiting for you to quit doing the very thing that stands between your plan for your life and His plan for your life. There is more abundance available for your life, and all that you need is already inside you—within Him.

Pick up your Shield of Faith. It's time to quit.

 **THE TRUTH**

"Quitting isn't failure. Quitting is freedom."

"YOU WERE TAUGHT, WITH REGARD TO YOUR FORMER WAY OF LIFE, TO PUT OFF YOUR OLD SELF, WHICH IS BEING CORRUPTED BY ITS DECEITFUL DESIRES; TO BE MADE NEW IN THE ATTITUDE OF YOUR MINDS; AND TO PUT ON A NEW SELF, CREATED TO BE LIKE GOD IN TRUE RIGHTEOUSNESS AND HOLINESS"

(Ephesians 4:22-24).

BRITTNEY TOLLINCHI

About the Contributor

BRITTNEY TOLLINCHI is a dynamic speaker, dedicated coach, passionate author, and inspiring podcaster known for her unwavering commitment to helping individuals make meaningful changes, uncover their inner greatness, and live authentically. As a warrior and truth-teller, she inspires actionable shifts in perspective and habits to reveal the light and abundance within each person. Brittney treasures her role as a purpose-driven mom and wife and brings profound relatability, infectious optimism, and lightheartedness to the complexities of balancing personal and professional life. She firmly believes God has a beautiful purpose for each of us, a plan far beyond our dreams, and she uses this belief to lead others to embrace their unique potential and live life to the fullest.

11

Follow Jesus and Walk on Water

By Ashley Weston

The Lie
"Go with Your Gut"

God radically changed the course of my life one Sunday night in January 2006. I said yes to an invitation to travel to Nicaragua for a short-term mission trip. It was a nice break from my nine-to-five management position in corporate America. On the airplane ride, I began reading the autobiography of the evangelist from Argentina who would be preaching for several nights during our trip. At the time, I was pretty comfortable with life. God had blessed me with success in business, a wonderful husband, a close-knit family, great friends, and health. My husband and I attended church regularly, and I read my Bible most mornings after a nice long run. But in reading the life story of this sold-out, on-fire evangelist, I realized my life and my faith were just that—my own. Also comfortable, secure, and, as painful as it was to admit it, lukewarm. I had never truly heard God speak to me until that moment on the airplane. I heard Him say, "Ashley, I don't want any of you if I can't have all of you." That moment pierced my heart as the fear of God washed over me in the best way possible, and I decided at that moment that I was going to be all in for Jesus.

Later that night, in the hotel room, as I was on my hands and knees praying and completely surrendering everything to the Lord, I did the hardest thing I have ever done in my life. I gave the Lord all of my heart. I confessed my past sins that spoke of shame and regret, surrendered all my hopes and dreams for the future, and lastly (and definitely the hardest), I gave Him all the anger and unforgiveness I carried from a childhood of rejection and abandonment that kept me in a continual prison of pain. After laying everything down at the foot of the cross and unable to cry any more tears, I drifted off to sleep.

Little did I know that the next day would mark me forever, as God was about to bless me more than I could imagine and change life as I knew it. We spent all of that day preparing for the evening event and helping the evangelist's team get ready to host hundreds of sick, hungry, and desperate people who lived in the surrounding areas of Nicaragua. The hope was to share the Good News of God's gift of salvation through a relationship with His Son, Jesus Christ, as Lord and Savior.

As day turned to night, the service began, and I found myself completely broken as I witnessed a hunger and thirst for God in these hurting people and a faith that was not only strong and completely confident but convicting and inspiring all at the same time. As the message of hope was preached, the evangelist shared the truth of Scripture that Jesus Christ was, is, and will always be Jehovah Rapha—the Lord our Healer. He invited anyone who was sick or hurting to pray and ask the Lord for healing. It was the most beautiful moment as these precious people took a leap of faith and believed God could do what His Word says. With tears of joy, compassion, and hope filling my eyes, I also took a leap of faith and put my hand on my back where scoliosis had been plaguing me for seventeen years, causing me pain and limited movements. The night ended, and my heart was filled with love as I witnessed the richest faith in some of the world's poorest people.

The next morning, as I was processing the amazing night of power, love, and God's presence, my hand moved to touch my back. In complete astonishment, I realized that God had performed a miracle—my back was straight!

Coming back from the mission trip, I was ready to leave my corporate nine-to-five behind to go share with the world what God had done and what He would continue to do if we had faith and believed. However, after praying and seeking the Lord's will, I heard Him again—and He told me to wait on His timing. Surrendering my will, my desires, and even my understanding of why, I waited seven years. God had called me to "trust in the Lord with all [my] heart and lean not on [my] own understanding" (Proverbs 3:5). I would like to say it was easy not going with my gut reaction and all the "godly" reasons I should leave and go serve Him right then, but it was a very long seven years.

Finally, the seven years came to an end, and I was ready to take that leap of faith into the unknown where God would call me. But in my immature reasoning, it didn't make sense. It would require leaving behind the comfort and security of finances as well as setting aside my family's heartfelt concern that I was making a mistake. But again, the Lord called me to "lean not on [my] own understanding." And so I jumped.

After six months of waiting for the Lord's direction, my faith wavered, and I gave into the lies of worry, doubt, and impatience. And yet, even in my weakness, God's faithfulness was strong. Little did I know He was about to perform another miracle and birth a company that would again change my life and impact hundreds of thousands of women all over America.

Coming from generations of artists, my mom and I always loved to do creative projects together. On one unremarkable summer day, my sweet mama bought some jewelry-making supplies and invited me over to experiment with creating earrings and a necklace. As I created my first clay medallion, I heard the Lord's voice instructing me, "Ashley, create a necklace medallion and inscribe your life verse on

"God's Word was faithful and true, and worry turned to peace, doubt turned to faith, and uncertainty became confidence!"

the back." So I wrote my beloved Proverbs 3:5: "Trust in the Lord with all your heart and lean not on your own understanding." I made this piece into a beautiful necklace, and as days passed by, it became a tool and reminder to trust God instead of trusting what I could see, feel, or understand. When my gut reaction was to worry, with uncertainty or doubt, I would grab this medallion around my neck, pray, and trust God instead of relying on my understanding. And as I did, the most amazing thing happened! The truth of the Bible became my reality. God's Word was faithful and true, and worry turned to peace, doubt turned to faith, and uncertainty became confidence! Another supernatural miracle had taken place in my heart, and I knew I had to share this tool with other women. As I suspected, I wasn't the only one battling worry, doubt, and uncertainty!

Three months later, before the first customer came to my makeshift home studio (i.e., my dining room table), the Lord spoke to me again, directing me in the budding business. I heard Him instruct me, "Ashley, I want you to pray and bless every woman who purchases jewelry." Okay, I thought to myself—no problem! However, as my first customer (and friend) shopped and was about to walk out the door, I felt that gentle nudge from the Lord. Would I go with my gut that was screaming, "No!"? Asking someone if I could pray for them seemed weird, and people don't usually mix prayer with business. But I knew the decision was mine. Would I trust God instead and surrender my understanding? After a moment that seemed like an eternity, I took a leap of faith and asked my friend if I could pray for her. Although she was very skeptical and hesitant, she agreed. As I closed my eyes and allowed the Lord to bless my friend, what poured forth from my lips was the Father's heart for His beloved daughter—pure love, acceptance, and presence. As we both opened our eyes and let go of each other's hands, I noticed tears streaming down her face as she thanked me.

She told me, "No one has ever done anything that special for me in my life." In a moment, those seven years of waiting on the Lord all made sense. This was what God had been preparing me for, and Hidden Truth Jewelry was birthed. That was February 17, 2016.

Looking back over the years, this wild adventure called entrepreneurship has had its ups and downs—the downs happening when my gut tried to understand God's ways and make a move without His leading. But God is faithful, and even when we stumble, He doesn't let us fall. It reminds me of Peter walking on water in Matthew 14:25–33:

> Shortly before dawn Jesus went out to them, walking on the lake. When the disciples saw him walking on the lake, they were terrified. "It's a ghost," they said and cried out in fear.
>
> But Jesus immediately said to them: "Take courage! It is I. Don't be afraid."
>
> "Lord, if it's you," Peter replied, "tell me to come to you on the water."
>
> "Come," he said.
>
> Then Peter got down out of the boat, walked on the water, and came toward Jesus. But when he saw the wind, he was afraid and, beginning to sink, cried out, "Lord, save me!"
>
> Immediately, Jesus reached out his hand and caught him. "You of little faith," he said, "why did you doubt?"
>
> And when they climbed into the boat, the wind died down. Then those who were in the boat worshiped him, saying, "Truly you are the Son of God."

As followers of Christ, we have the choice to stay in the boat because our gut tells us walking on water is impossible, or we can take that leap of faith when Jesus calls (even though it might seem crazy) and experience supernatural walking on water. And when life's storms distract us, make us doubt, and once again tempt us to lean on our gut reactions, rest assured that Jesus is right there to keep us from drowning.

My gut told me not to wait seven years and to quit my job immediately because it seemed like the right thing to do. My gut told me to stay in my job when seven years finally came because it wasn't a smart financial move. My gut told me to listen to my family because they only had my best interests in mind. My gut told me to doubt God because His timing wasn't "on time." My gut told me not to mix my faith with business. My gut told me people would think I was weird, and I would lose the sale if I asked to pray for them. My gut told me I was my own boss and should make my own decisions without praying about them. My gut told me so many things . . . but if I had listened, I would have missed out on the most exciting journey only God could be the author of.

If you truly want to see God do the supernatural in your business and your life, you will need God's armor covering you as well as His most powerful weapon—the Sword of the Spirit. Walking on water and seeing God do even greater things than you can ask or imagine requires using the Sword of the Spirit, which is the Word of God. Listen daily to the whispers of the Holy Spirit, and then act upon them. Read and meditate daily on the Word of God and be obedient to it. In any and every situation, the Sword of the Spirit will not only destroy the lies of the enemy aimed to make you sink but it will lead you to "walk on water," such that everyone who witnesses will give God the glory!

> "If you truly want to see God do the supernatural in your business and your life, you will need God's armor covering you as well as His most powerful weapon—the Sword of the Spirit."

Below are suggestions that will help you pick up the sword, trust God, and start walking on water!

1. Spend time with the Lord every day. Worship Him! It's amazing the supernatural exchange that happens when we worship God

and focus on Him. What seemed like problems will suddenly shrink in His presence, and joy, peace, and hope will renew your heart. Talk to Him! Prayer is just a conversation with Jesus! If you want to build a successful Kingdom business, have the mindset that Jesus is CEO and ask Him for wisdom (James 1:5). He will help you make decisions that bear much fruit in your business and have an eternal impact that changes lives forever. Read His Word! Remember, you are armoring up every day, and the Word is your weapon. When you read, He will highlight certain words or verses. Meditate on those and take them with you as you go throughout your day. You'll be equipped for anything!

2. Let go of what's popular, what other people may think, and what culture advises is "wise." Remember, if you are building a Kingdom business, you are walking by faith and not sight (2 Corinthians 5:7). If you are feeling the struggle of wanting to go with your gut because it makes more sense, stop, pray, and ask the Lord for His perspective about the situation. Be expectant that He will provide wisdom and then be bold to obey what you hear. Pick up your sword and trust God.

3. View your business as a vehicle to glorify God and advance His Kingdom while serving others as your first priority. Then God will provide everything you need and give you the desires of your heart. Matthew 6:33 says, "But seek first his kingdom and his righteousness, and all these things will be given to you as well." Use God's Word, i.e., the Sword, as a lamp to your feet and light to your path (Psalm 119:105). Jesus is the Word and the way, truth, and life (John 14:6). And remember, let God lead and define what success looks like.

4. Don't get distracted by the wind and the waves; instead, keep your eyes on Jesus. The storms of life will come, and the opportunity for doubt, discouragement, and fear will arise to tempt you, but remember that God's ways are higher than our ways and His thoughts higher than our thoughts (Isaiah 55:8–9). So keep your eyes on Jesus and keep walking on the water even

when it doesn't make sense. In those moments when fear wants to grip your heart, ask God for guidance through His Word.

5. Enjoy the journey. Goals and milestones in business are wonderful, but we can easily make that our focus. As a Kingdom entrepreneur, each day has blessings of its own, and you may miss them if you're not present in the now. Life-changing miracles are on the table each day that you say yes to following Jesus and trusting His plan for your business and, ultimately, your life. It may feel like climbing a mountain some days but don't miss the beautiful, fragrant flowers He's planted along the way for you to enjoy and give away to other weary travelers.

Going with your gut is a belief that your gut (or heart) is a compass inside you that will direct you to your "true north" if you dare to follow it. But as we see in Jeremiah 17:9, "The heart is deceitful above all things and beyond cure. Who can understand it?" Our hearts don't tell us the truth; they only tell us what we want. So don't go with your gut; follow Jesus. When you do so, you won't ever have to wonder what it feels like to walk on water because your life and your business will be the most exciting adventures of supernatural faith!

So listen for God's leading, and then go, jump, take that leap, and find out for yourself what Peter experienced—the most exhilarating journey of walking toward Jesus that his gut definitely could not understand—supernaturally walking on water!

 **THE TRUTH**

Stop, pray, and ask the Lord for His wisdom.

"TRUST IN THE LORD WITH ALL YOUR HEART AND LEAN NOT ON YOUR OWN UNDERSTANDING"

(Proverbs 3:5).

ASHLEY WESTON

About the Contributor

ASHLEY WESTON, a.k.a. the Jesus cheerleader, is super passionate about sharing the *joy* of the Lord with everyone she meets! She is a wife, a mother to two amazing kids, and the founder of Hidden Truth Jewelry, a jewelry line that clothes women with God's powerful Word. Ashley is also the author of the best-selling art-devotional book *I Am Who You Say I Am*, written to remind women of their identity as God's beloved daughters. Ashley loves spurring on women of all ages and stages, reminding them of the amazing adventure Jesus offers in an intimate relationship. Ashley is so passionate about sharing the hope of Jesus with people because He radically changed her life and miraculously healed her of scoliosis in 2006. She wants people everywhere to experience the same tender yet powerful touch of the Lord too!

12

The Power of Authenticity

By Dr. Chelsea D. Washington

The Lie
"You Have to Be Someone Other Than Yourself to Succeed"

"Be louder; be bolder." "Just jump right in there!" "Can you do it more like her?" "Can you say it like he did?" These are just a few examples of the relentless pressure I've faced throughout my life. Each time these words echoed in my ears, they seemed to chip away at my unique qualities, leaving me feeling unsure of myself and often causing me to retreat both mentally and emotionally. It was as if the world told me my introversion was a flaw, a roadblock to my dreams and success. I know many of you have experienced this, and I want you to know that these words pushed us further away from our true selves. This struggle is real, and it's time we acknowledge it.

As introverts, we thrive on alone time, value deep connections over surface-level interactions, and find energy in solitude. Yet our society often glorifies and praises the extrovert ideal, leaving introverts feeling inadequate. This societal narrative suggests that being extroverted is the only way to make a significant impact, leading many, like me, to believe they must be gregarious, energetic, and constantly in the spotlight to succeed. This societal ideal clashes with my personal story and how I view and understand the world.

My love for solitude, small groups, and one-on-one encounters is where my energy and creativity flourish. So how have I achieved academic and business success without trying to transform or become someone I am not? This chapter dispels the myth that extroversion is the *only* path to success. I will show you that true success lies in authentic living by drawing from biblical examples, practical strategies, and my lifelong journey as an introvert navigating an extroverted world. You can be successful without compromising your authenticity. This realization may bring a sense of relief and empowerment, knowing that you can thrive in your unique way.

My Journey to Authentic Living

There was a time when I believed that to be successful, I had to be the "life of the party." Yet I felt uncomfortable and out of place whenever I found myself in spaces where that ideal was expected and often demanded. As someone who naturally gravitates toward quieter, more reflective settings, I found this expectation exhausting and unfulfilling. There was a season in my career when it was a part of my role to attend networking events regularly. I worked very hard trying to put on a façade of extroversion. While I was putting forth my best effort, what was displayed to the outside world appeared awkward and often disingenuous.

After leaving networking events or large functions, I made a beeline for my car. When my feet finally hit my front door, I felt drained, irritated, and, frankly, darn lousy about myself. Ruminating on each encounter, I asked myself, "Why can't I thrive in these environments, like some of my peers? Why can't I wave a magic wand before each social gathering that would allow me to 'turn on' and move through the crowds, smiling, laughing, and making small talk? What is wrong with me?"

This internal conflict continued for many years until, one day, I had a revelation. I was at a business event with nearly two hundred people where I was supposed to "make connections" and "get people interested in our services" (another daunting task, to say the least). Instead, I ended up conversing with one of the participants on the outskirts of the crowd.

But there was something different about this particular encounter. We engaged in a deep, meaningful conversation about our work, passions, and faith. Not only were we connecting on a deeper level, but I realized that what I was sharing was making an impact. The person asked me questions and was interested in knowing more about me, my journey, and my company's services. After the conversation, I felt highly energized and connected, something I had never experienced at previous events. That encounter was a turning point for me. It made me realize that my source of strength comes from deep connections and thoughtful reflection, not from being the center of attention or standing in the middle of a crowd or "working a room" of hundreds of people.

From that moment on, I embarked on a self-acceptance journey that wasn't about fitting into a mold. I sought guidance from fellow introverts and learned how to walk in my Kingdom authority as an introvert. For me, this meant understanding and embracing the unique strengths and perspectives that introversion brings while delving into God's Word to understand more about what They (Father, Son, and Holy Spirit) said about me and how I could be successful—not an easy task. This journey was filled with self-compassion and seeking God's guidance, which provided me with comfort and reassurance.

Over time, my belief system changed. My character and even the way I carried myself slowly shifted. I started to understand the truth of who I am and that I was created with intentional thought and purpose. I saw the creative power in being introverted and realized that my calling might not be for the masses but for the missed. So, one person at a time, I focused on building meaningful relationships and creating spaces where I could thrive and others could be seen.

Surprisingly, my career flourished as a result of embracing my authentic self. I discovered that by being true to myself, I could bring my best self to my work and make a more significant impact than I ever could by pretending to be someone I wasn't. Embracing my introverted nature not only allowed me to connect deeply with others and foster genuine relationships, but it also created a fulfilling career, empowering me in ways I never thought possible. I also want you to experience this joy and fulfillment by embracing your authentic self.

The more I embraced my introverted nature and valued who I was, the more I realized I needed to be more intentional in my interactions. So I sought our Divine Creator's guidance and wisdom and did what God said. Let me repeat that: I did what God told me to do. His guidance and wisdom are always there for us introverts to lean on, providing comfort and reassurance in our journey toward authentic living.

I set boundaries by saying no to specific social and professional obligations, exploring self-care practices, and cultivating a support system that nourished me. I avoided situations that left me feeling drained and unfulfilled. I increased physical activity, particularly nature walks and yoga. I explored and sought opportunities more aligned with my strengths and passions. I made sure to carve out time to recharge my battery after being around large groups, empowering myself to live life on my own terms.

In the Bible, there are many examples of individuals who achieved great things through quiet strength and introspection. Moses, for instance, was not a natural-born speaker, yet he led the Israelites out of Egypt. His success didn't come from being the loudest or the most outgoing, but instead, it came from his faith, determination, and ability to listen to God's guidance. Similarly, introverts can find their unique path to success by embracing their true selves and trusting their innate and God-given abilities.

The Myth of the Extrovert Ideal

The idea that extroversion is the key to success is deeply ingrained within many aspects of our society. From how we conduct business meetings to the social structures in educational institutions, the extrovert personality is often celebrated and rewarded. And though these extroverted qualities provide valuable contributions to society, the same can be said of introverts, who are frequently disregarded and minimized. The profound impact that quiet reflection, deep thinking, and careful listening have on personal and professional success is often overlooked.

We must not forget the impact introverts, from Albert Einstein to President Obama and Rosa Parks to Eleanor Roosevelt, have had on society and the world. Without these introverts and their leadership, the world would not be the same.

The same is true in a biblical sense. Although the Bible does not boldly call these individuals "introverts," we know that they exemplify the characteristics of introversion.

Biblical Examples of Introverted Leaders

The Bible contains examples of introverts who achieved great success and fulfilled God's purpose for their lives. These stories remind us that God values authenticity and has a unique plan for each of us, regardless of our personality type.

"...God values authenticity and has a unique plan for each of us, regardless of our personality type."

Moses: The Reluctant Leader
One of the most compelling examples of a successful introvert is Moses. When God called Moses to lead the Israelites out of Egypt, Moses expressed his insecurities about his speaking abilities and leadership qualities. In Exodus 4:10, Moses says to the Lord, "Pardon your servant, Lord. I have never been eloquent, neither in the past nor since you have spoken to your servant. I am slow of speech and tongue."

Despite his self-doubt and perceived limitations, Moses became one of the most influential leaders in biblical history. His leadership was not characterized by extroverted charisma but by obedience, humility, and a deep reliance on God. Moses's story illustrates that God's plans for us do not depend solely on our natural abilities or personalities but on our willingness to trust Him and live authentically.

Mary: The Quiet Reflector
Another example is Mary, the mother of Jesus. In Luke 2:19, after the shepherds visited and shared the angel's message about her newborn son, it is written, "But Mary treasured up all these things and pondered them in her heart." Mary's quiet reflection and deep contemplation did not diminish her significance. Instead, it highlighted the power of inner strength and faith. Mary's role in God's plan was profound, and her story shows us that quiet reflection and deep faith can be just as powerful as outward expressions of strength.

Nehemiah: The Strategic Planner
Nehemiah is another biblical figure who exemplifies the success of living authentically. As the cupbearer to the Persian king, Nehemiah was not a natural public speaker or a charismatic leader. However, when he learned about the destruction of Jerusalem's walls, he was deeply moved and sought permission from the king to rebuild them.

Nehemiah's approach was methodical and strategic. He spent time in prayer and careful planning before taking action. His success came from his ability to efficiently organize, plan, and execute the rebuilding project. Nehemiah's story demonstrates that strategic thinking and careful planning (often associated with an introverted personality) can lead to remarkable achievements.

Jesus: The Epitome of Leadership
Jesus exemplified introverted leadership through His profound moments of solitude and reflection, which guided His public ministry. Often, Jesus withdrew to isolated places to pray and seek communion with God, as seen in Luke 5:16: "But Jesus often withdrew to lonely places and

prayed." His leadership was marked by deep, thoughtful interactions rather than loud proclamations. In the Sermon on the Mount (Matthew 5–7), He delivered powerful teachings in a calm, contemplative manner, emphasizing inner transformation over outward appearances. By balancing quiet introspection with impactful public actions, Jesus demonstrated that authentic leadership stems from a deep inner connection with God and a genuine, thoughtful approach to guiding others.

Practical Strategies for Living Authentically

Living authentically means embracing who you are and leveraging your unique strengths. It involves recognizing that your value and potential are not determined by how extroverted you are, but by how true you are to yourself and your God-given purpose. Here are some practical strategies to help you live authentically and achieve true success.

1. Embrace Your Unique Strengths

Every individual has unique strengths and abilities. Instead of conforming to societal expectations, focus on identifying and developing your strengths. Reflect on what makes you unique and how you can use those qualities to meaningfully contribute to your personal and professional life.

Practical Strategy: Create a strengths inventory. List the skills, talents, and qualities you believe set you apart. Reflect on past experiences where these strengths have helped you succeed. Use this inventory as a guide to navigate your career and personal growth. If you are still trying to figure out where to start, you can find personality and strengths-based inventories online to guide you. Some churches, employers, and universities offer these personality and character assessments at no cost.

Spiritual Insight: Once your skill sets have been identified, ask the Lord to show you how They (Father, Son, and Holy Spirit) want you to use your strengths to advance the Kingdom.

2. Prioritize Deep Work

Introverts often excel in deep work—focused, uninterrupted tasks that require concentration and thought. This type of work can lead to significant achievements and is highly valued in many fields.

Practical Strategy: Designate specific times in your day for deep work. Eliminate distractions and create an environment conducive to focus. Use techniques, like the Pomodoro method or time blocking, to maintain productivity.

Spiritual Insight: Dedicate time to studying and reading the scriptures to deepen faith practices and understanding.

3. Build Meaningful Relationships

While extroverts may thrive in large social settings, introverts often find fulfillment in profound, meaningful relationships. Focus on building and nurturing strong connections with a few individuals rather than spreading yourself thin in large social circles.

Practical Strategy: Invest time in nurturing relationships with people who support and uplift you. Engage in one-on-one or small group interactions where you can connect more deeply. Remember, quality is better than quantity in relationships.

Spiritual Insight: Spend dedicated time with God, fasting and praying, deepening your connection and relationship with your heavenly Father. The more time you spend with your heavenly Father, the more intimate your relationship will become.

> "The more time you spend with your heavenly Father, the more intimate your relationship will become."

4. Leverage Your Listening Skills

Introverts are often excellent listeners, an invaluable skill in personal and professional settings. Good listening can lead to better understanding, stronger relationships, and more effective problem-solving.

Practical Strategy: Practice active listening in your interactions. Listen for understanding rather than focusing on what you will say in response. Focus on the speaker, avoid interrupting, and provide thoughtful responses. Use your listening skills to build rapport and trust with others.

Spiritual Insight: Tune your spiritual ear, listening for the Holy Spirit's whisper in every circumstance and asking for guidance and instruction every step of the way.

5. Practice Self-Compassion

It's easy to feel inadequate when comparing yourself to extroverted peers. Practicing self-compassion involves treating yourself with the same kindness and understanding you would offer a friend.

Practical Strategy: Develop a self-compassion routine. When you engage in negative self-talk, pause and reframe your thoughts positively. Remind yourself of your worth and the unique contributions you bring to the table.

Spiritual Insight: Find out what God says about you, your character, and why He created you. Knowing how valuable you are to the Creator shifts how you treat yourself.

6. Seek God's Guidance

Living authentically as a person of faith involves seeking God's guidance and trusting in His plan for your life. Prayer and meditation can provide clarity and direction, helping you to stay true to your God-given identity.

Practical Strategy: Incorporate regular prayer and meditation into your daily routine. Use this time to seek God's wisdom and guidance, asking for strength to live authentically and fulfill His purpose for your life.

Spiritual Insight: Praise and worship the Divine Creator, making it a part of your daily routine. Praise and worship prepare your heart to receive and hear from God.

Prayer

Lord, thank you for guiding my steps today and for being a
constant friend and leader.

I choose to trust you every step of the way.

Help me live authentically and courageously,
knowing my talents and gifting and using them for your glory.

Give me the courage to say yes, even when I'm scared,
and to say no to what you don't desire for me.

May your voice be the loudest among the noise around
me and a gentle whisper in the quiet.

Thank you in advance for answering my prayers.

Amen.

Conclusion

The myth that extroversion is a prerequisite for success is just that—a myth. True success is not about fitting into a specific mold but embracing yourself and living authentically. It is about putting on the Belt of Truth, the truth of who you are as your heavenly Father created you. Drawing from the examples of biblical figures, like Moses, Mary, and Nehemiah, we see that God values and uses all personality types for His purposes.

Success comes from recognizing and leveraging your unique strengths, prioritizing deep work, building meaningful relationships, maximizing listening skills, practicing self-compassion, and seeking God's guidance. By living authentically, you can achieve true success that aligns with your values and fulfills your God-given potential.

So let go of societal pressures and embrace your authentic self. Trust that your Creator has equipped you with everything you need to succeed, just as you are. And remember, even if you find yourself in the corner at a party, you may be precisely where you're meant to be.

By sharing my story and these strategies, I hope you are inspired to embrace your authentic, introverted self. Success doesn't require us to be someone we're not. It demands that we understand and leverage our unique gifts from our Divine Creator. True fulfillment comes from living authentically by putting on the Belt of Truth, honoring who we really are, and finding joy in our life journey.

In a world that often celebrates extroversion, let's remember that introverts have a valuable and necessary role. Our quiet strength, deep connections, and thoughtful insights can create a lasting impact. So embrace your introverted nature, live authentically, and trust that your unique path to success is just as valid and fulfilling.

 **THE TRUTH**

"I am made in the image of my Creator. I have unique gifts and talents that will propel me exactly where I am meant to be."

"ALL PRAISE TO GOD, THE FATHER OF OUR LORD JESUS CHRIST, WHO HAS BLESSED US WITH EVERY SPIRITUAL BLESSING IN THE HEAVENLY REALMS BECAUSE WE ARE UNITED WITH CHRIST. EVEN BEFORE HE MADE THE WORLD, GOD LOVED US AND CHOSE US IN CHRIST TO BE HOLY AND WITHOUT FAULT IN HIS EYES. GOD DECIDED IN ADVANCE TO ADOPT US INTO HIS OWN FAMILY BY BRINGING US TO HIMSELF THROUGH JESUS CHRIST. THIS IS WHAT HE WANTED TO DO, AND IT GAVE HIM GREAT PLEASURE. . . . FURTHERMORE, BECAUSE WE ARE UNITED WITH CHRIST, WE HAVE RECEIVED AN INHERITANCE FROM GOD, FOR HE CHOSE US IN ADVANCE, AND HE MAKES EVERYTHING WORK OUT ACCORDING TO HIS PLAN"

(Ephesians 1: 3–5, 11, NLT).

CHELSEA WASHINGTON

About the Contributor

DR. CHELSEA, a trailblazing entrepreneur, consultant, and leader, has forged a distinctive path in wellness and self-care. As the innovative founder and "chief self-care doctor" at My Ohm Wellness, LLC, she brings a unique blend of qualifications as a therapist, executive well-being consultant, and self-care and life transformation coach, with a special focus on somatic approaches that set her apart.

Dr. Chelsea's odyssey toward wellness and self-care is a compelling testament to the transformative power of self-healing. Triggered by a life-altering diagnosis of lupus, this experience not only reshaped her outlook on life but also sparked a profound spiritual, mental, emotional, and physical transformation with the Divine. These transformative practices now underpin her approach to serving others, offering a beacon of hope for those embarking on their own wellness journeys.

Having refined her expertise in personalized settings over the years, Dr. Chelsea is poised to share her invaluable insights with a global audience. Through her highly acclaimed podcast *Divine Centered Meditations*, speaking engagements, corporate well-being programs, one-on-one coaching, and courses, she meets participants at every stage of their wellness journey, guiding them toward a healing process meticulously tailored to their unique needs.

Dr. Chelsea's unwavering commitment to others' well-being is the driving force behind her work. Her mission is to assist individuals in managing negative stressors and anxiety, empowering them to create the life the Divine has called them to have—a genuine, connected, and unique expression of abundance. This steadfast dedication to wellness sets her apart and reassures clients of her commitment to their journeys, inspiring trust in her services.

WHAT NOW?

BELT OF TRUTH

In Roman culture, the belt on the soldier's tunic was where his sword hung, which gave him freedom of movement. The belt was the foundation of the soldier's armor – holding his sword and his breastplate. Before we speak, do, or make decisions, as "businestry" (business + ministry) leaders we must check our belt of Truth! Before you speak or decide, pray and ask Holy Spirit what God's TRUTH has to say about this situation or relationship.

Ephesians 6:14,
John 14:6, John 8:32
1 John 3:18, John 16:13

What's the lie?

What's the truth?
(the bible verse and/or biblical figure that represents the truth)

What tool/tactic/strategy/resource will you arm yourself with to be victorious?

BREASTPLATE OF RIGHTEOUSNESS

Once a Roman soldier fastened his belt, he would then strap on his breastplate. The breastplate — a large bronze shield, covered his midsection from the soldier's neck to his thighs. The purpose—to guard vital organs — especially the HEART. Without the breastplate, a soldier was vulnerable to attacks. It could mean the difference between life and death. Do a safety check with Holy Spirit. Are you allowing Him to work in you, producing fruits of righteousness?

Proverbs 4:23-27, Ephesians 4:1-16, Psalm 139, Matthew 15:8

What's the lie?

What's the truth?
(the bible verse and/or biblical figure that represents the truth)

What tool/tactic/strategy/resource will you arm yourself with to be victorious?

SHOES FITTED WITH PEACE

Roman soldiers, wore shoes called "caligae". These were heavy military-like sandals — half boot, half sandal. These sandals were the sign of an equipped soldier and one ready to move. It was common that soldiers would march 25 miles. Soldiers needed firm footing to concentrate on the battle at hand. So make ready your feet, put on The Gospel of Peace that comes from the Good News so that you will be fully prepared!

Ephesians 6:15, John 16:33, Matthew 5:9, Colossians 3:15, John 14:27

What's the lie?

What's the truth?
(the bible verse and/or biblical figure that represents the truth)

What tool/tactic/strategy/resource will you arm yourself with to be victorious?

SHIELD OF FAITH

Fiery darts were one of the most dangerous weapons in ancient warfare! In Paul's time, warriors would carry huge oblong shields soaked in water! When a fiery arrow was shot, the arrow sank deep into the saturated wood, and the flame was extinguished. This is what FAITH does in our battles. What lies, doubts, and fears do you need to extinguish today with your shield of FAITH?

Proverbs 3:5-6, Mark 11:22-24, Romans 10:17, 2 Corinthians 5:7, Ephesians 6:16

What's the lie?

What's the truth?
(the bible verse and/or biblical figure that represents the truth)

What tool/tactic/strategy/resource will you arm yourself with to be victorious?

HELMET OF SALVATION

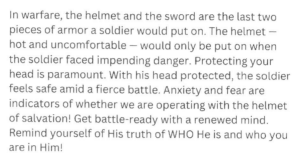

Isaiah 12:2, John 14:6, Ephesians 2:8-9, Romans 8:38-39, John 3:16-18

In warfare, the helmet and the sword are the last two pieces of armor a soldier would put on. The helmet — hot and uncomfortable — would only be put on when the soldier faced impending danger. Protecting your head is paramount. With his head protected, the soldier feels safe amid a fierce battle. Anxiety and fear are indicators of whether we are operating with the helmet of salvation! Get battle-ready with a renewed mind. Remind yourself of His truth of WHO He is and who you are in Him!

What's the lie?

What's the truth?
(the bible verse and/or biblical figure that represents the truth)

What tool/tactic/strategy/resource will you arm yourself with to be victorious?

SWORD OF THE SPIRIT

Every Roman Soldier knew it took a good offense to win a battle. Their weapon in close combat was called the gladius. The gladius was a short sword that inflicted more damage than larger swords and it was easier for him to handle in battle. Paul noted only one offensive weapon—the soldier's sword. Today as Jesus Followers, our sword is the Spirit and the Word of God. We can never win the battles of life without God's Holy Spirit and His Word.

See how Jesus used the "sword" as He battled.
Matthew 4:1-11
Ephesians 6:17,
Hebrews 4:12,

What's the lie?

What's the truth?
(the bible verse and/or biblical figure that represents the truth)

What tool/tactic/strategy/resource will you arm yourself with to be victorious?

ACKNOWLEDGEMENTS

Without the F.I.T. Press team, this book would be words without binding, left in the minds and hearts of brilliant entrepreneurs.

Candice - you're the ultimate myth-buster. Thank you for being a truth-teller and calling this project into its highest level of service to others by not just busting the lies, but a keen attention to building the warriors in the process.

Becky - your ingenuity and creativity help bring life to our big dreams and off-the-wall ideas. You cement them with your imagination by co-laboring with Christ to reveal His message through every project.

Sharon - your commitment to every word blesses our writers and honors God. Your attentiveness and passion for these projects breathe confidence for the authors and our ultimate message.

The Joy-full Entrepreneurs - as this series continues, we honor each author who has raised their hand to the mission and shared their wisdom with the world through these pages. You make ABBA proud every time you testify of Him in who you abide and ultimately produce the fruit of joy!

The F.I.T. in Faith community that stands united as one, representing the body of Christ through their expression of God on the earth, celebrating and sharpening one another through His word and gifts.

GET CONNECTED DEEPER!

Tune in for a quick hello video from the author!

International Speaker, 7x # 1 Best Selling Author, Top 1% Podcaster & Marketplace Minister

A serial entrepreneur who works with high capacity Christian leaders to turn their messages into movements and share the Good News!

TAMRAANDRESS.COM

Your story doesn't just matter for you, it matters to move others!

1 CHRONICLES 16:24 (NLT)
Publish His glorious deeds among the nations.
Tell everyone about the amazing things he does.

A Christian Publishing House dedicated to turning messages into movements. On mission to mobilize the critical voices for such a time as this. Specializing in co-hort compilations, to make way for writers to collaborate with other prolific members of the Body of Christ. Our works open conversations around mental, physical, relational, financial and spiritual health and wholeness journeys, often directly associated to our rooted identity and purpose driven life.

Learn More & Don't Wait to Get Published!

Ladies! Beauty Awaits from the inside-out and outside-in.

We will explore every detail of God's wondrous creation. Starting with YOU! This wellness retreat is an immersive experience intended to get you back to the basics (mind, body, and HOLY spirit) by heightening your senses to what matters most: your vertical alignment, so you can horizontally serve, share, and SHINE!

Fella's! The Great Outdoor Awaits! Embark. Elevate. Expand. Explore.

Getting primal to perform at our highest potential as men, husbands, fathers, and leaders by activating our sonship. Join us on this "unforget-table, epic, and life-changing" adventure that will catalyze you to exist in your power, authority, and passion.

Contact: hello@thefoundercollective.org

let's find out your

PROFIT INDENITY

Reveal Your Passion and Spiritual Gifts
Connection to Start & Grow Your Business

TAKE THE QUIZ TODAY!

HAVE YOU EVER WONDERED?

What your purpose is?

How you could use your giftings as a global messenger for God?

How your spiritual gifts are connected to your prosperity?

How your passion propels your profit?

This is a podcast for the messengers!
The called ones.
The mobilized ones.
The ones on a mission to turn their message into a movement.

This show was designed for Declaring Truth, Transforming Narratives & *Catalyzing Christians to Speak, Write, Build & Testify*.

SUBSCRIBE & LEAVE A REVIEW FOR A SHOUTOUT ON AIR!

JOIN THE

F.I.T. in Faith Network Resource Hub!

IT'S TIME TO ACTIVATE YOUR *god dream*

DOWNLOAD NOW!

The F.I.T. in Faith Network Resource Hub will serve as a growth tool for you as a Fierce Female ready to Fight The Good Fight.

SPEAK, WRITE, BUILD, TESTIFY

Count this app as your Aaron and Hurr on your fulfilling and sometimes hard days of blazing the trail of your purpose-driven calling.

- **SOUND BIBLICAL BUSINESS SUPPORT - COURSES & CONTENT**
- **TRAINING & IMPLEMENTATION TOOLS**
- **TEMPLATES**
- **QUICK START RESOURCES**
- **FINANCIAL TRAJECTORY PLANS & MODELS**
- **COMMUNITY CONNECTIONS - FOCUS GROUPS**
- **LIVE OFFICE HOURS MONTHLY WITH Q&A AND ON THE SPOT COACHING**

This is a movement of empowered legacy building, chain breaking, pioneers, liberating others to stand in freedom, firm in their identity, and activating authority as Kingdom citizens. Join the movement today.

WE ARE THE MOBILIZED CHURCH!

Are you already operating as a Joy-full Entrepreneur and want to partake in our next compilation project?

Or perhaps you want to take a deeper dive. Get a hold of Vol. 1 & 2 in our series where we unpacked Principles, Power and Presence - vol. 1 & Solutions, Signs, & Wonders - vol. 2

ABOUT THE AUTHOR

Get ready to meet Tamra Andress! She's a 7x #1 best-selling author featured in Forbes, USA Today, and other well-known publications. Tamra's a keynote speaker, top podcaster with over 500 episodes on The Messenger Movement Podcast, and co-host of The Founder Collective and Girls Gone Holy Podcasts too. As an ordained minister, she is passionate about helping Christian leaders turn their messages into movements to further catalyze the Good News. Her company, F.I.T. in Faith Press, turns dreams into reality through publishing, podcasting and platform development —all while keeping play at the heart of it! Her non-profit is gearing up to launch a world-class Academy ordaining and sustaining marketplace ministers alongside partners like Ford Taylor in 2027. When she's not on a mic, she's adventuring with her family somewhere tropical, nose deep in a book or doing cartwheels to keep life fun with her hubby of 12 years and 2 kiddos!

Made in the USA
Columbia, SC
13 February 2025

53777405R00124